*Whenever a sign is present, ideology is present too.
Everything ideological possesses a semiotic value.*

Valentin Volosinov

*Branding has moved so far beyond its commercial
origins that its impact is virtually immeasurable in
social and cultural terms.*

Wally Olins

*Society cannot share a common communication
system so long as it is split into warring classes.*

Berthold Brecht

*Never cover the letter R so that the brandmark
reads FEAPLESS.*

Filnders University 'Fearless' Style Guide

*My weariness amazes me,
I am branded on my feet*

Bob Dylan

HOW TO COUNTER

1. Fundamentalist

2. Marketplace

3. Semiotics.

Customer Analysis

Trends

Brand

Unmet needs

Segmentation

Brand involvement

BRAND IDENTITY

FIGURE 1 | Conceptual model

Total articles reviewed
(n=100)

Flexibility / Diversity

FIGURE 3 | Personal branding model.

Brand as
product

ted the emergence and penetration of the concept—personal
ent discourse. Among the key is a widespread shift of the
areers from organizations to individuals (Arthur and Rousseau,
and Kossek, 2014). Indeed, business ...
time workers out of jobs, e.g., because of the "greening" of the
... in the call centers, and because of the advances in artificial
... brand-oriented approaches (based upon the ... 1997

a. What is

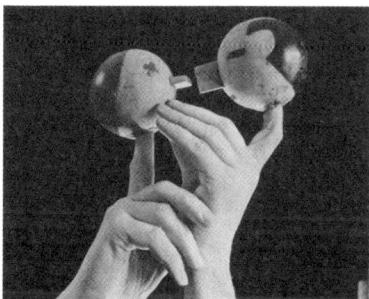

b. Post-Branding?

Writing, creative conceptualisation and curatorial by Jason Grant and Oliver Vodeb
Design by Inkahoots and Oliver Vodeb
in Meanjin (Brisbane) and Naarm (Melbourne), Australia

inkahoots.au
memefest.org

Printed by Printon in Estonia

Published by Set Margins' in The Netherlands, 2023
setmargins.press

ISBN: 978-90-832706-7-8

Original image sources, previous pages: *The Readers Digest Do-it-yourself Manual*, Readers Digest, Aus, 1972; *Personal Branding: Interdisciplinary Systematic Review and Research Agenda* by Sergey Gorbatov et al, November 2018 Frontiers in Psychology 9 (November):1-17; *The Influence of story-telling on the consumer-brand relationship experience* by Cátia Fernandes Crespo, Alcina Gaspar Ferreira & Ricardo Motta Cardoso, Journal of Marketing Analytics, 2022; *Historical Evolution and Spread of Branding & The 3 Dimensions of Post-branding* by Inkahoots and Oliver Vodeb in Post-Branding Explainer for Greenpeace, Inkahoots, Aus, 2020; consciousbrandsreport.com; *Puppetry Today* by Helen Binyon, Studio Vista Ltd, UK, 1966.

What is Post-Branding?

How to Counter Fundamentalist
Marketplace Semiotics

By Jason Grant and Oliver Vodeb

What is the harm of branding? Here branding is revealed as a symptom and catalyst of scorched earth capitalism. Following are 20 reasons to quit branding.

01.

01 -
DIS-
BRANDED

pg 18

01

Introduction

Exit:

Are you a designer doing branding? Pull the plug.

Are you a professor teaching branding? Put away the PowerPoint.

Cancel the curriculum. Rescind the industry.

Quit the soul-sucking quicksand of branding's corporate scheming.

Amidst rampant precarity, stagnant wages, rising costs, housing and healthcare in crisis, branding helps designers pay the bills. But spiraling adversity and inequality are just enabled and exacerbated by branding. Here branding is an insidious neoliberal project of self-sabotage.

Branding dilutes democracy. The public sphere is colonised, dialogue is simulated and monopolised and our natural and mental environments are monetised.

Then what's left?

Branding is the sacred communion of corporations and consumers that seeks to transubstantiate everything, from the connection between governments and citizens, to the trusted conversations between friends, and the whispered declarations between lovers.

Brands are promoted and accepted as legitimate tools to differentiate products and services whose characteristics are very often homogeneous. Branding is promoted and accepted as a neutral process when actually there is little it doesn't frame and distort.

02

Branding's domination of creative industries

Hijacked:

The relationship between production and consumption is changing. With neoliberal capitalism, the old forms of value creation in traditional workplaces are being replaced with a mediated process of social interaction and communication, converted into economic value via the brand.

Brands aren't just intruding on culture, they *are* our culture. They are the sponsored mechanisms for constructing and manipulating meaning and human identity. Brands don't just want our loyalty, they want our love, they want our-*selves*.

The communication industries have been hijacked. The rapid rise of modern branding is plain to see with the increase of graphic design studios either identifying as branding agencies, or including branding as their key service – for example, in Australia, from almost none prior to the year 2000, to around 85% in 2022 (AGDA).

Design studios have devolved into branding agencies because the money is easier. Advertising agencies were already gone. Neither (want to) understand the risks of their fundamentalist marketplace semiotics.

Meanwhile, the planet floods and burns. Research and innovation are distracted by the substantial resources invested in branding, promised improvements in products and services are deferred while their promotions get sleeker and slipperier, and we're left empty handed, or with fistfuls of literal junk.

03

Branding's unacknowledged historical origins

Sordid History:

The historical application of the term 'branding' from livestock, slave, prisoner, and then product identification, to the expression of corporate and personal values, has a consistent trajectory. The recent semantic shift from terms like 'design' and 'visual identity' to 'branding' was necessary to define an increasingly dehumanising process.

Branding is as much a totalitarian as a totalising ideology, with its authoritarian intolerance of any values existing beyond its grasp.

Although there's a reluctance to acknowledge it, the Swastika and its omnipresent applications in 1930's Germany saw the historical genesis of fully realised systematically programmed and documented, modern branding methodology.

Branding's popular consolidation was in the first decade of the new millennium, and its pre-eminence came in the wake of the Global Financial Crisis, (almost a decade after Naomi Klein's *No Logo*), when previously unshakable faith in free-market superiority was eroded. This newfound ideological insecurity combining with rapidly developing digital technologies was the perfect impetus for the growth of less tangible and more abstract forms of capitalism. Economic data for Europe and the United States shows intangible investment overtook tangible investment in 2008, around the time of the Global Financial Crisis. The most significant financial assets of many of the world's biggest companies are not their physical products, services and infrastructure, but rather the altogether more nebulous concepts of models, brands and algorithms. All this is by design.

04

Branding's rewriting of history

The Branding of Branding:

Coca Cola introduced the tentative beginnings of a standards manual in 1929 to guide the company's transition from drinking fountains to bottling. In 1936 the Nazis published the hefty *Organisationsbuch der NSDAP*, a branding blueprint covering many aspects of Nazi public communication. This prototype style guide/ organisational handbook is an equally likely candidate for the field's foundational document.

A lot of slippery side-stepping goes into denying the extent of Nazi influence on branding's evolution. For example, if you're trying to discover who made the first brand manuals, you'll read vague claims about the German designer Peter Behrens instigating 'a systematic design programme' for German company AEG from 1907 – without any evidence of an actual brand manual (despite being cited in texts about brand manuals). So the established, yet likely mis-leading, implication regarding Behrens's, and others', role in this history serves to underplay the pivotal role of Hitler's murderous aesthetic ambitions, and therefore the grievous reality of branding's biography.

But reality can't compete with branding's boasts. A show at London's Design Museum, curated by global brand consultancy Lipencott, announced that the whole of biological evolution is the evolution of branding, and that cave paintings "are an important demonstration of how our Homo Sapien ancestors were hard-wired to brand". While Wally Olins wrote that under Napoleon, "the whole of France was rebranded". The official milestones of branding's history are just flagrant attempts at rendering branding inevitable: the brazen branding of branding.

05

The homogenising role of branding

Diversity Morons:

Branding is reductive and homogenising. It bullies difference and diversity.

The famed modernist graphic designer Massimo Vignelli explained it best when writing about branding manuals: "Anyone who says that a manual is a creative straitjacket is a moron. Without a manual you will end up speaking a dialect. A good manual allows you to speak a language."

Speaking a pure language and barring dialects is great, just ask any colonialist looking for a reliable, time-honored weapon of domination.

Perhaps they never fully appreciated their legacy, but like the Nazi-fleeing modernist émigrés before them, Vignelli (who began visiting the United States from Italy in 1957) and his cohort became strident enablers of design's role in facilitating USA post-war capitalist hegemony. And they weren't alone in accusing messy diversity of "threatening culture".

This idea that "we all live in single world, a One-World world," as Arturo Escobar puts it: "is largely conceived of from the perspective of the Euro-American historical experience and exported to many world regions over the past few hundred years through colonialism, development, and globalization." Branding can't tolerate the Zapatista dictum, "a world where many worlds fit."

06

Branding's assault on civic entities

Trojan Horse:

Branding's reconstitution of non-corporate entities as market-tamed subordinates is causing real harm. Branding has become an ideological Trojan horse, invading social and cultural realms traditionally resistant to corporate influence.

This process is more destructive than conventional co-optation. Co-optation *uses* non-corporate entities, as a parasite uses its host – the host is harmed but survives because the parasite needs the host for its own survival. Branding, however, can violently colonise these spaces, and attack the host's fundamental ethos, so even radically independent or oppositional agendas are displaced, transformed and debased.

In 2012, Food Connect Sydney, a branch of the ground-breaking Australian community supported agriculture initiative, parted ways with the founders after it was gifted a marketing mentorship with a bank. With its newly acquired branding expertise, the Sydney branch rejected a proposed campaign critical of corporate food systems for being too 'activist' (and not adhering to perceived brand guidelines), consequently exposing a new, irreconcilably antithetical ethos.

Branding acts here as a disciplining tool through coercion and punishment, leaving just enough freedom to extract profit for those who control the branding and are its soldier servants.

Then conversely with co-optation, corporations' appropriate social meaning so brands become the medium through which capital is socialised. Either way, with passive co-optation or active assimilation, branding, as a form of neoliberal 'common sense' is a site of urgent political struggle.

07

Branding's limiting of critical thought

Codifying Cliché:

As a vanguard of late capitalism, the creative industries affect the cliché of denouncing clichés – only to systematically process and police clichés through draconian branding methodologies.

Aesthetic unoriginality though is the least damaging feature of cliché. In his book *Thought Reform and the Psychology of Totalism: A Study of "Brainwashing" in China*, Robert Jay Lifton writes: "The language of the totalist environment is characterized by the thought-terminating cliché. The most far-reaching and complex of human problems are compressed into brief, highly reductive, definitive-sounding phrases, easily memorized and easily expressed. These become the start and finish of any ideological analysis."

Branding is ruthlessly cultivated corporate cliché. Syme in Orwell's *1984* says: "Don't you see that the whole aim of Newspeak is to narrow thought? In the end we shall make thoughtcrime literally impossible, because there will be no words in which to express it".

Most commercial communication is cliché – slogans, soundbites, propaganda – but branding is an increasingly dominant system of codifying and enforcing this 'thought-terminating' corporate rhetoric. And when there's nowhere to hide from free-market culture, there's nowhere left to think freely. Or to misquote McLuhan in *From Cliché to Archetype*: "The more the brands record about each one of us, the less we exist".

08

Branding jargon & 'thought-reform'

Brandspeak:

Branding blurs the line between persuasion and coercion. There's the promise of reward with a moral appeal to our potential amidst inescapable seductive spectacle, and the threat of punishment with market defeat for businesses, obscurity for civic organisations, or precarity for individuals.

These facets of 'thought-reform' (Lifton) are intrinsic to branding. The entire process, from initial conceit to public dissemination, is built on a reductive, totalist lexicon in an atmosphere of real social and economic anxiety.

For so-called 'creative' practices, branding agencies' evidence of actual creativity is thin. The monotonous, interchangeable clichés they use to describe their own businesses, and the very branding they design, are typically generic language templates so limited in scope, depth and self awareness, they could easily be mistaken for parody. Linguistic constriction promotes chronic jargon ('imagination', 'creativity', 'disruption'...), as banal platitudes – advertising difference but achieving exactly the opposite.

As an apparatus of 'milieu control', Brandspeak is key to a doctrine that requires, not just conformity and the rewriting of history, but through regulation of internal and external communication, a moulding of the subject to fit the myth. As Lifton puts it when discussing the 'brain-washing' of political prisoners: "This undermining of identity is the stroke through which the prisoner 'dies to the world', the prerequisite for all that follows."

09

Branding's inextricable link to ownership

Violent Possession:

A protester holding an I AM A MAN sign. A crowd carrying BLACK LIVES MATTER banners. Taking a knee during the national anthem. Pussy Riot's balaclavas. Hong Kong pro-democracy protesters' umbrellas…

These radical signifiers have all been claimed as brands. But they are freely shared symbols. They are critiques of power. They are language. They are culture. They are ideas that can build movements. They can not be owned by a corporation or even by a protesting individual. This distinction as an obvious definition of branding (branding is inextricably linked to ownership) is now often overlooked. However non-corporate entities ignoring this dimension of branding are vulnerable to hostile ideological assimilation.

Though it is often claimed that branding has evolved beyond its original constitution (beyond ownership to 'belonging') sophisticated contemporary branding methods are animated by virulent foundational principles. Branding persists as a strategic system of exclusive property rights enforcement. This is as true today as it was when enslaved humans were violently branded with obscene symbols of possession.

Any civic or activist organisation adopting branding, or framing their public communication as branding, needs to reckon with this enduring feature of branding's character. Branding affirms the authority of capital regardless of its host's mission.

Post-branding is proposed as a strategic alternative, defending the commons, and countering branding's hierarchical and exclusive ownership.

10

The tensions in activist groups over branding

In a Bind:

Civic organisations can be wary of corporate communications foiling their missions. There are often tensions within activist and socially focused groups over branding.

For example, when we surveyed the members of a major global environmental organisation about the value and appropriateness of branding, contradictions emerged.

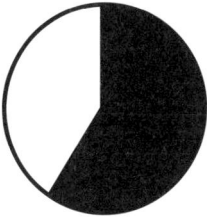

59% of people thought their organisation should adopt visual communication methods (commercial marketing and branding methods) that are used by for-profit corporations.

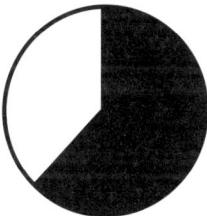

However, a similar number of people (62%) thought that branding conflicts with their organisation's culture and values, and could misrepresent the organisation's identity. What do these contradictions tell us about branding?

11

The naturalisation of branding

The Air We Breathe:

Businesses (and Governments, and others) now look to brands for their internal organising principles. Branding for public interests is not just 'consumer facing', it is internally absorbed and often manifested as a demoralised in-house culture, and at worst as a debased common good.

In spite of branding's insistence on its role as broad-casted 'authenticity', an organisation's hallowed, incorporated mission-statements increasingly derive from cynical public advertisements.

And 'authenticity' is not the big problem here. Branding's disorientation of desire and moulding of myth doesn't just promote an inauthentic life, it materialises exploitative, extractive relations that threaten life. Alternatively, with post-branding, visual communication can: "devalue people's investment in systems, products, services and lifestyles that defuture, while at the same time, generate new ambitions and material desires bonded to life-affirming futures." (Fry)

Branding though is just more proof of capitalism colonising language while taking advantage of its principles. Because the very principle of language will put 'the brand' as a primary signifier in the centre of exchange of meaning between people, 'the brand' and branding seem to be unavoidable. Branding has therefore become naturalised. It has become an orthodoxy that seems as natural as the air we breathe, and therefore so difficult to imagine alternatives. To misquote Fredric Jameson: "It is easier to imagine an end to the world than an end to branding."

12

The extraction of economic value via communication

Exploitation:

Brand management is just coercive strategies of intervention in 'consumer freedoms', creating obstacles to exercising and experiencing freedoms: "in ways different from those prescribed by the particular ambiance." (Arvidsson) A controlled or regulated freedom shapes the context in which freedom is exercised.

Branding operates on the affective level, exploiting our emotions, deploying various strategies to create a false sense of reality. To produce value, branding manipulates our need for identification by creating a culture through which we maintain myriad minuscule inter-personal competitive differences. Because this can be done indefinitely, a sense of a shared life is eroded. How can we resist effectively if we are exploited in ways that ensure it is harder and harder to relate to each other? One obvious solution is that we can resist through understanding, which is acquired through education. Unfortunately, branding is also a key instrument in capitalism's grand project of knowledge destruction.

Branding is a key form of 'communicative capitalism' (Dean). Instead of exploited labour under industrial capitalism, now any act of communication (especially on monopolised digital platforms – a Google review, a tweet, an Instagram post) has the potential to become free labour that is brandable and transformable into economic value. It is this process which also destroys the meaningfulness of communication. Real political action and transformation is subverted by communicative capitalism exploiting communication. In this sense, abolishing branding is revolutionary.

Branding and competition

Never-Ending Race:

Branding is a product of competition and technology that sees the world as a never-ending race. The more competitive an organisation, the more it employs branding strategies. A fascinating example: we know a university where the head of the university, in any of her public addresses, always wears clothes in the colours of the corporate brand.

You can also recognise these places by their excessive use of the words 'innovation', 'creativity' and 'performance'. In this sense branding is also complicit in the change of one of our primary activities. We don't work anymore, we perform. We don't go to workplaces, but to performance centres.

No wonder managers and university heads love branding. Branding is the market's 'creative' adversarial imperative, constantly reinforcing self-interested individualism over solidarity. The neoliberal surge of brand-bolstered competitiveness has optimised consumption at the expense of any collective resistance to social inequality and economic disadvantage.

#14

Branding's framing of values & social participation

Minding Our Business:

By collecting and using audience information to strengthen the relationship between the brand and their audiences, brands operate as tools of surveillance capitalism – with their ownership and control of channels for social participation, and the power to shape people's behavior.

Because brand management defines the limits and nature of freedom, the possibilities for genuine political action and social transformation are undermined.

Branding doesn't just mind our business, it breeds the very mindset we resist and challenge. Market values squeeze out non-market values. As George Lakoff puts it, those using the frames and language of their opponents are more likely to adopt their values: "Their words draw you into their worldview."

In this world, when all you have is branding, everything looks like a brand. But if we stop framing basic human communication – and communication between actors whose primary motivation is not indefinite short term profit – as 'branding', we can more successfully promote our own values on our own terms.

#15

Branding's concealment of social & political conflict

Branded Away:

Branding is now what we call entrenched strategies of aestheticising the concealment of social and political conflict.

To do branding is to obscure and reinforce hierarchies of privilege and class division. The branded, neoliberal unreal *real* is always constructed at the expense of the *real* real. Everyday political realities hide behind the rictus grin of a staged neoliberal reality – an endless enforced entrepreneurialism, where people's lives are shattered by a program of privatised, reduced or withdrawn essential social services and welfare support. Branding, as a weapon of neoliberal instrumentality is complicit in embedding institutional inequality and disadvantage.

For example, in our formerly working class neighbourhoods of West End in Brisbane, and St Kilda in Melbourne (Turrbal & Yuggera and Boon Wurrung land long before that), all the messy contradictions of rapid gentrification, such as evictions, homelessness, violence, substance abuse and addiction, the shrinking of the public realm and erosion of supportive community are utterly disregarded, and in effect denied and enabled by branding. Instead, we are presented with branded commercial development promoting vapid templates of frictionless aspirational cosmopolitanism.

Branding has breached the last barriers to advertising's voracious environmental and psychological penetration. The heretofore-stubborn evidence of coercive corporate power, of real social and political antagonisms, is hereafter elegantly branded away.

16

The congenital masochism of self branding

Social Media?:

Branding can be a product of debt as a primary instrument of social control. In an indebted world people are forced into a precarious existence. Under these conditions people become 24/7 one person enterprises. The 'entrepreneur of the self' creates themself as a brand. Social media exploits this. Facebook, as the biggest advertising medium in human history, is a perfect example. Many Facebook users are carefully curating themselves as brands.

We know someone who said that all people are brands. And that instead of using their names, we should simply refer to them as brands. This person was a Chair of a media and communications department at an Australian university.

We also know someone who, during a discussion about the importance of focusing on the social implications of communication, asked: "When you say social, do you mean social media?" This person was Chair of a design department at an Australian university.

The strategic damage of advanced capitalism is not only dangerous delusion, but is also stupidity at the expense of knowledge.

17

Branding and addiction

Tiny Bits of Pleasure:

What branding doesn't capture through its spectacular media presence it conquers through addiction.

It is complicit in the ever-increasing precarity of workers, as tenuous short-term contracts leave people with few choices other than to self-brand. Rather than making workers less precarious, this merely teases economic benefit. The curation of the self-brand is a constant task performed largely through 'digital housekeeping'. What we post, what we like, who we connect with, and what we share becomes our brand.

These self-branding activities are enforced by technology designed to exploit our longing for experiencing pleasure. Because pleasure is an episodic phenomenon – it never lasts long – we try to reinforce and repeat actions which give us pleasure. Tiny bits of pleasure, which we experience if our posts get liked and shared, glue us to the screen. The extent and the nature of our engagement with these technologies determines our addiction. When we are worthless in the market, self-branding generates an illusion of self-worth. And capitalism sells the limitless engagement with such technology as 'freedom'.

The work required to produce a self-branded subject is not a matter of choice. The individual's productivity becomes the lens through which they see the world. The flexibility becomes the culture of their actions, and the technology enables them to perform in a time space continuum that is deterritorialised and instant. Through the extraction of value and the disciplining of the subject, the totality of branding has reached its performative optimum through addiction.

18

Branding, managerialism & human centred design

Understanding
the Human:

Branding, managerialism and 'human centred design' together conspire to withdraw our autonomy. Managerialism is the most extreme and exploitative strain of management. Its role is to bully and control employees in order to endlessly extract value and transfer wealth and power upwards. 'Performance management' is the main tool used by managers to burden workers with unrealistic expectations and create a system of constant and permanent audit, underpinned by feelings of professional inadequacy. The worker is not trusted to do the work, instead they are forced to obey performance expectations translated into numerical values – abstract governance by .xls spreadsheet!

We have reached branding's new horizon, a wave of branding which incorporates the organisation's structure, reasons for being, and their internal and external relationships. Here branding shifts from being the voice of an organisation to being the very values and discourse themselves.

So called 'human centered design' is often the method by which managerialism as a form of governance is integrated into an organisation. Human centered design wants to "understand the human" by importing concepts from social sciences and humanities. These design concepts have grown popular in business schools and among managers. Branding penetrates such organisations vertically as well as horizontally, and gives them meaning and symbolically legitimises them inwards and outwards into a unifying whole.

19

Branding's debasement of communication

Implosions:

Communication now has less 'use value', and more empty 'exchange value'. In constant pursuit of profit, the messages are no longer as important as the speed and quantity of their circulations.

Under current capitalism, communication implodes because, by definition, communication happens when a message also generates a response. But, increasingly this does not happen. Messages circulate without response in an endless data stream: "zero comment" (Lovink). But branding remains central to this process; on digital networks, where people self-brand, it is the driver of the messages created.

As much as branding tries to persuade us it is the most necessary, important and powerful form of communication, in more and more cases branding happens when communication collapses into itself.

Meanwhile, with complex algorithmic automations, artificial intelligence is increasingly used by branders to expedite creative assets and messaging. It's not just AI's labor efficiencies that excite corporations, it's also the ability to outsource human morality, ethics and agency.

On the 84th anniversary of the Nazi led "Night of Broken Glass", KFC Germany aplogised for a bot-generated, automated push notification that translates as: "It's memorial day for Kristallnacht! Treat yourself with more tender cheese on your crispy chicken. Now at KFCheese!"

20

Conclusion

Entry:

Branding is not isolated. It is a product, symptom and catalyst of capitalism. But creating meaning around signifiers, through a process of meaningful exchange like communication does not have to be predatory.

Can we imagine an alternative method of communicating collective identity that supports the common good? Can we abandon the brandwagon? Can we imagine post-branding?

Though branders may dismiss it as 'utopian', or 'naive', or as an 'activist aesthetic', post-branding is a change at the root of how and what we know – how we imagine the world and do things in it as designers. We need to wade through branding's shallow depths and simplistic complexities. Why is branding being taught in universities with no real alternative? Why are design awards rewarding branding? Is branding merely a compensation, an attempt to hype a terminally boring culture?

Commercial forms of communication are based on 'external authority'. It is the image, the appearance – as a brand and branding device – which help legitimise and enable extractive cultures. Can we instead design as if all the world wasn't just a shopping mall and all its citizens targeted competitive consumers? A collective identity can create relations which include the interdependencies, needs and desires of a broad constituency, rather than the exclusive priorities of a minority corrupting power.

Post-branding is new set of strategies embedded in a new culture of craft. A new way of being and knowing, for a new way of relating with the world.

Following is an index of images illustrating and extending the preceding text. They urge your time and attention towards translating their interconnected and overlapping signs, visual echoes and mirrored messages. Here is a general chronology recalling branding's material past, derelict history, fascist tendencies, and tactical vulnerabilities...

02. MIXED MESSAGES

pg 60

IAMES NAYLOR

Of all the Sects that Night, and Errors own
And with false Lights possesse the world, ther's none
More strongly blind, or who more madly place
The light of Nature for the light of Grace.

708

I E J T

A Q

t

M- N

M K L

Ex

D K M

2 J

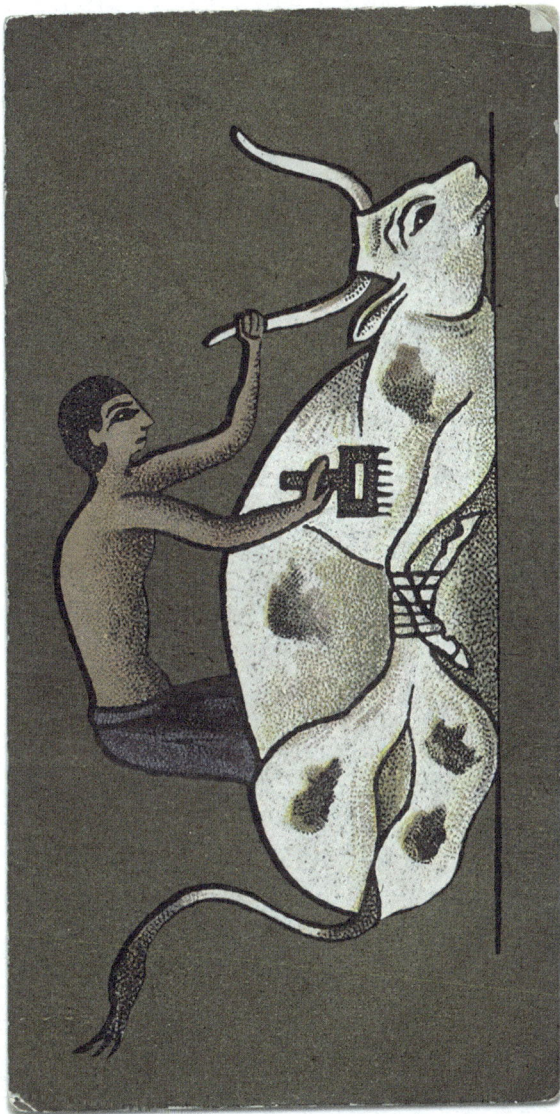

BRANDING A NEGRESS AT THE RIO PONGO

From a wood engraving in Canot's *Twenty Years of an African Sla*
New York, 1854

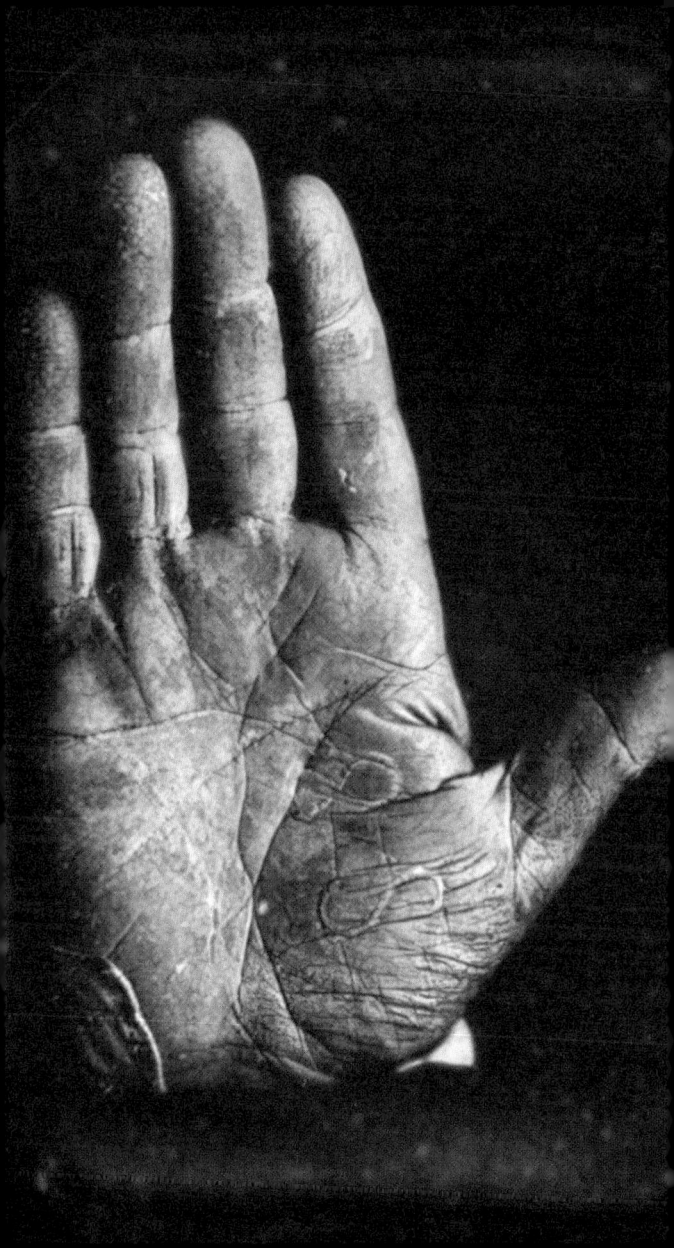

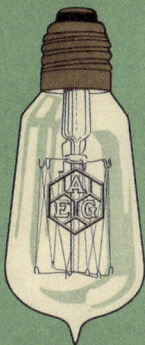

AEG

Metalldraht-Lampe

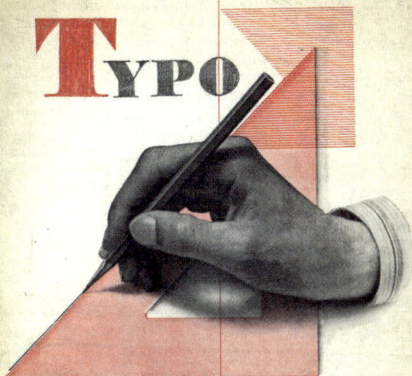

Organisationsbuch
NSDAP.

Herausgeber:
Der Reichsorganisationsleiter der N

1936

Zentralverlag der NSDAP., Franz Eher Nachf..

Kraftwagen-Stander
Dienststander

Reichsleitung

Reichsleiter

Hauptdienstleiter, Hauptamtsleiter u. Amtsleiter

Gauleitung

Gauleiter

Stellvertr. Gauleiter u. Amtsleiter

Kreisleitung

Kreisleiter

Amtsleiter

Tafel 18

Kraftwagenstar

Gegenstücke zum Dienststander

Armbinden

Pol. Leiter, SA., NSKK.
DAF.-Werkscharen, NSBO.
Parteischulen
Reichsarbeitsdienst

Hitler-Jugend

NSD.-Stu

Graphic Design
Guide

single element that will surely
and cause our work to be
here . The IBM logotype
expression of our company's
ity that of identifying,
tensing authority whenever
fied mailer, advertising, TV
signs, vehicles, and
s denominator which helps
ess material.

NO LOGO®

NAOMI KLEIN

Life is easier on iPhone.

And that starts as soon as you turn it on.

Everything Amazon sells is delivered with ease, so we took their existing frown and turned it upside down. The once generic line became a simple arrow curved into the shape of a smile. This was distinctive, worked at any scale, and gave a human face to a corporate giant. The letters A and Z appeared in the name and provided a gift. The smile of the arrow could show, quite literally, that they sold everything from A to Z.

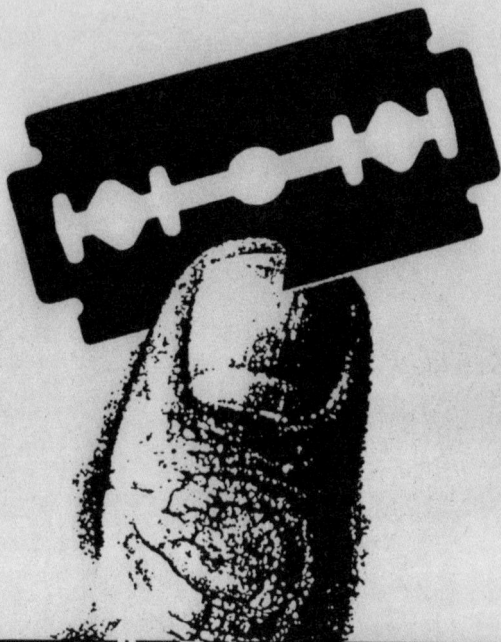

Stoppt die Folter.

amnesty international
Kampagne gegen die Folter
Spendenkonto 30-3417

ai

92

STOP THE DEATH PENALTY:
THE WORLD DECIDES

130 countries have abolished the death penalty in law or practice.

Now the United Nations General Assembly will vote on it.

It is now time for a worldwide end to capital punishment. Join us in campaigning for global abolition.

www.amnesty.org/deathpenalty

AMNESTY
INTERNATIONAL

WORLD
COALITION

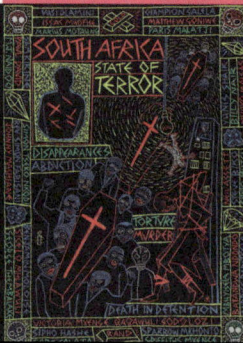

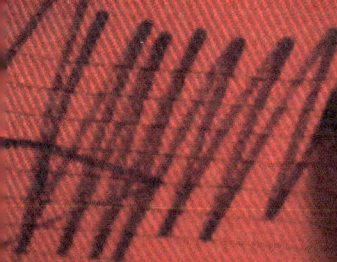

Carl T. Bergstrom
@CT_Bergstrom

I posted a photoshop of the golden Trump statue (left) into the famous photo of evangelicals praying over Trump (right).

I thought the reference was clear, but it's causing confusion. I've deleted.

AFAIK, no one prayed over a golden Trump statue. In public, anyway.

March 1st 2021

47 Retweets **339** Likes

ing genocide

celebrating genocide

celebrating genocide

KFC
celebrating genocide

ing genocide

celebrating genocide

KFC
celebrating genocide

KFC
celebrating gen

ting genocide

KFC
celebrating genocide

KFC
celebrating genocide

KFC
celebrating gen

KFC
ating genocide

KFC
celebrating genocide

KFC
celebrating genocide

KF
celebrating gen

KFC
ting genocide

KFC
celebrating genocide

KFC
celebrating genocide

KFC
celebrating gen

KFC
ating genocide

KFC
celebrating genocide

KFC
celebrating genocide

KFC
celebrating gen

FC
ting genocide

KFC
celebrating genocide

KFC
celebrating genocide

KFC
celebrating geno

Daniel Sugarman
@Daniel_Sugarman

···

In a successful attempt to outdo Brewdog in the "Worst Marketing Blunder of the month" stakes, KFC Germany reportedly sent out a push notification offering customers special chicken deals for Kristallnacht, before sending out another message apologising. Absolutely hideous.

🔴 KFC Germany ⌃

🔴 5 min ⌃

SORRY, UNS IST EIN FEHLER PASSIERT
Durch einen Fehler in unserem System haben wir eine inkorrekte und nicht angemessene Nachricht über unserer App verschickt. Dies tut uns sehr leid, wir werden unsere internen Prozesse umgehend überprüfen, damit dies nicht noch einmal passiert. Bitte entschuldige diesen Fehler. Team KFC

🔴 1 h ⌃

Gedenktag an die Reichspogromnacht
Gönn dir ruhig mehr zarten Cheese zum knusprigen Chicken. Jetzt bei KFCheese!

1:39 AM · Nov 10, 2022 · Twitter for iPad

101

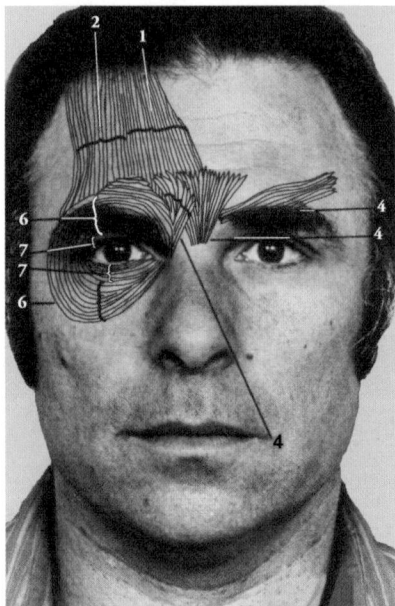

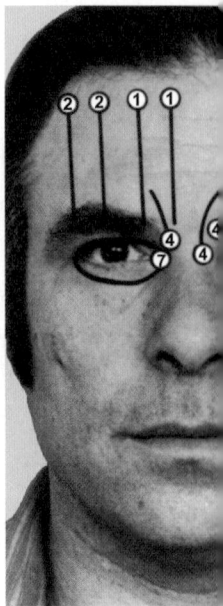

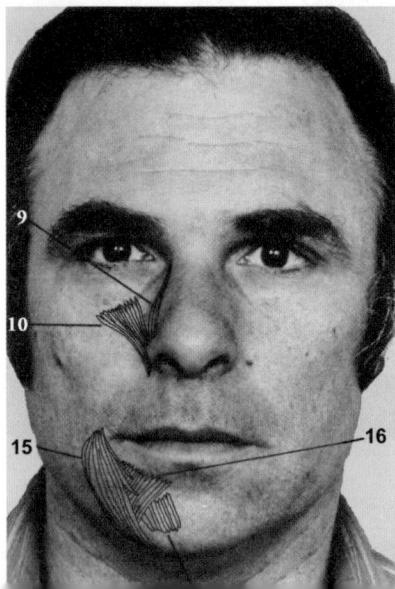

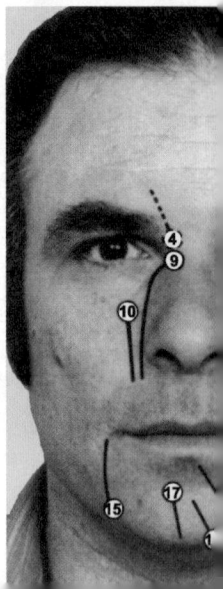

ments

ent
d

Funding

ips

Strategy

ee
quired)

nes

ntacts

Home > Research > Research development

Research development

Research development at City is led by the Deputy Vice-Chancellor (Research and International), Professor Dinos Arcoumanis, supported in particular by Jo Braiford Ramberg in the Centre for Research and International Development, by colleagues Research and Enterprise Unit and by the University Research Committee.

The research development section of the website contains information about contract University activity and events in support of research. If you are not able to find what looking for, please contact us.

Research students should also look at the research degrees web pages.

Research Grants and Contracts Office (City network log-in and password required. The Research Grants and Contracts Office is a part of the City Research and Enter (CRED). Its main functions include the provision of assistance to academic staff one financial and contractual aspects of submitting applications for research funds and managing research grant and contract income once obtained, and the dissemination information about opportunities for obtaining research funds. The Research Grants Contracts web pages include information on grant application procedures, links to Research Council and other useful websites, and monthly reports on grant applicant and obtained.

IBM E 44123

TIME CARD

MO.	DAY	YR.
PERIOD ENDING DATE		

RATE

EMPLOYEE NAME

JOB TITLE

INITIALS | FED. STATE | TAX CLASS.

AUTH-
CODE

	HOURS	GROSS EARNINGS ✦	SOCIAL SECURITY ✦	FEDERAL TAX ✦	STATE TAX ✦	NET EARNINGS ✦

AGENCY CODE

	SUN.	MON.	TUES.	WED.	THURS.	FRI.	SAT.

APPROVED: _____

(left margin, vertical) C 1 2 3 4 5 6 7 8 9 10 11 12 13 14 15 16 17 18 19 20 21 22 23 24 25 26 27 28 29 30 31 32 33 34 35 36 37 38 39 40 41 42 43 44 45 46 47 48 49 50 51 52 53 54 55 56 57 58 59 60 61 62 63 64 65 66 67 68 69 70 71 72 73 74 75 76 77 78 79 80
SOCIAL SEC. NO. | INTLS. | EMPLOYEE NAME | JOB TITLE | AUTH. | ACCOUNT CODE | RATE | HOURS | DAY NO. | GROSS | F.I.C.A. | WITHHOLDING TAX | NET

(right margin, vertical) RATE | EMPLOYEE NAME | JOB TITLE | SOCIAL SECURITY NUMBER | GROSS EARNINGS | F.I.C.A. TAX | FED. W. TAX | STATE W. TAX | NET

VIRGINIA COMMONWEALTH UNIVERSITY

Insert Draw Page Layout Formulas Data Review View

f_x Name

	B	C	D	E	F	G

School of Design Academic Workload All

Name		Staff Number	
Academic Level	LEVEL C	Time Fraction	1.00
Discipline	Communication Design	Total Workload Hours	1,656
AWAM Manager			

		Detail
s for variation to standard (select where applicable)		

	Weeks	Hours
Annual Leave *(adjust if necessary)*	4	144
...ional Leave *(enter detail)*		0
Total Leave Planned		144

Academic Workload Model 2022 for detail	Total Hours	Weeks	Percentage Workload	2022 AWA...
COURSE DELIVERY *(enter below)*	725	20.13	43.8%	
...ERS BY COURSEWORK SUPERVISION *(enter below)*	0	0.00	0.0%	
HONOURS SUPERVISION *(enter below)*	0	0.00	0.0%	45 - 65%
OTHER TEACHING ACTIVITIES *(enter below)*	55	1.53	3.3%	
TEACHING & TEACHING RELATED ACTIVITIES			47.1%	
HDR SUPERVISION *(enter below)*	#VALUE!	#VALUE!	#VALUE!	
RESEARCH & SCHOLARSHIP / PHD	414	11.50	25%	25 - 40%
RESEARCH, SCHOLARSHIP & HDR SUPERVISION			#VALUE!	
...ROGRAM MANAGEMENT *(enter on PM calculator)*	0	0.00	0.0%	
...TERNAL ENGAGEMENT/LEADERSHIP *(enter below)*	149	4.15	9.0%	
EXTERNAL ENGAGEMENT *(enter below)*	224	6.21	13.5%	5 - 30%
ENGAGEMENT			22.5%	
TOTAL YEAR	#VALUE!	#VALUE!	#VALUE!	98 - 102%

...VERY, COORDINATION & ASSESSMENT	Course (select) *search list by typing part of course code or title*	Credit Points	Semester
	GRAP2081 - Design Studies (Comm Design)	12	Sem 1
	GRAP2081 - Design Studies (Comm Design)	12	Sem 1
	GRAP2627 - Research Design & DigitalMedia	12	Sem 1
	GRAP2627 - Research Design & DigitalMedia	12	Sem 1
	GRAP2627 - Research Design & DigitalMedia	12	Sem 2
	GRAP2627 - Research Design & DigitalMedia	12	Sem 2
	GRAP2626 - Design Strategy	12	Sem 2
	GRAP2764 - Design & Digital Prof Prac	12	Flex
	COMM2784 - Prof Res Project (Comm Design)	24	Sem 2

...TERS BY COURSEWORK SUPERVISION	Enter detail	# Semesters	# Students	Total Hours
			Total	0

...earch Lookups | **AWAM Tool** | Academic Workload Framework 202... | Research Plan | Engagement Plan | Summary fo...

Flinders University under fire over "shameful and stupid" move against leading academics

Editor: Melissa Sweet **Author:** Melissa Sweet Monday, October 25, 2021

In: Global health, Health inequalities, Public health, Social determinants of health

Health leaders are shocked and dismayed by a Flinders University proposal to close the Southgate Institute for Health, Society and Equity, and to "disestablish" the positions of key staff, including the Institute's director, Professor Fran Baum.

Global and national leaders in public health have written to Flinders University stating their concerns about the proposal, and stressing their support for Baum and colleagues, warning that the university faces reputational damage.

The plans were revealed to Southgate staff recently as part of a restructuring of the College of Medicine & Public Health (outlined here in a Flinders University statement to Croakey today), and a further announcement is expected tomorrow (26 October) following a consultation period.

In a letter to Flinders, Professor Ron Ronald Labonté, Distinguished Research Chair in Globalization and Health Equity at the University of Ottawa, said he had worked with Baum and colleagues for decades and had "long regarded Flinders as an ethical and socially responsible upstart representing the best of modern, humane, and engaged academic scholarship".

"This no longer appears to be the case," he said. "With regret, sadness, and profound shock, I hereby resign my affiliation with Flinders University."

Speaking truth to power

Liz Harris, Adjunct Associate Professor at Centre for Primary Healthcare and Equity UNSW, and another long-term collaborator of Southgate, told *Croakey* she was in shock when she heard the news, which indicated the precarious situation facing academics and the undermining of the independence of universities.

"My sense is if she's vulnerable to dismissal, then we're all vulnerable to dismissal. If you've got someone who's bringing in millions of dollars in NHMRC and AHMRC grants, and who's led Australia in qualitative research and the social determinants of health, and who can find themselves left afloat, then who is safe?"

Harris said the case was a reminder that "you can't afford to speak truth to power without consequences", and that "Flinders Uni should reflect on the long-term damage to their reputation".

en Fearless is being used as a CTA
th the brand mark (i.e. Find your
rless), Circular should be used as the
porting font. The text size for the copy
ompanying "Fearless" should be bigger
n the sub copy (i.e. "Apply for study in
2") to ensure a hierarchy of messaging.

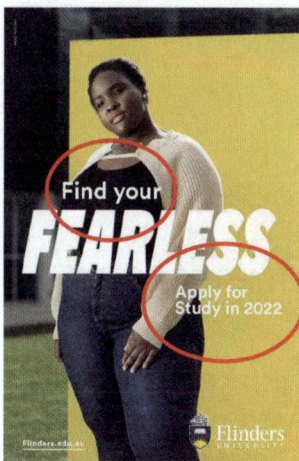

Find your **FEARLESS**

Apply for
Study in 2022

Flinders.edu.au

Flinders UNIVERSITY

ders University - *Fearless*

Find y
FEA

Flinders.edu.au

YLE GUIDE

EXECUTION EXAMPLE GUIDES - Study Area

study area communications,
re the Fearless brand mark is
applied, Circular should be used
headlines.

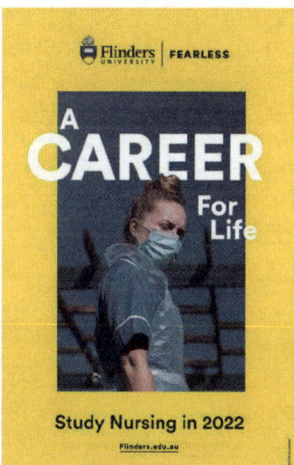

Flinders UNIVERSITY | **FEARLESS**

A
CAREER
For
Life

Study Nursing in 2022

Flinders.edu.au

Flinders UNIVERSITY

A
CAR

Study Nu

107

Dictionary
of
NEWSPEAK

DLS: A Common Language

Design Language System

...n Design Language
...stem (DLS)—from its
...principles to color palettes—
...is the foundation of every
product we ship at Airbnb.

Good morning from Australia! 🧡
Here's a little reminder to make time for the things you love today.
..... for no other reason than that it makes YOU happy. 😄 🌕 🐺

You deserve it.

#... **See more**

👍❤️ 2.2K   23 comments 16 shares

👍 Like   💬 Comment   ↪ Share

Most relevant ▾

Write a comment...   😊 📷 🎞️ 🎲

Press Enter to post.

👑 Top fan
Jutta Dixon

What it is is beautiful.

Have you ever seen anything like it? Not just what she's made, but how proud it's made her. It's a look you'll see whenever children build something all by themselves. No matter what they've created.

Younger children build for fun. LEGO® Universal Building Sets for children ages 3 to 7 have colorful bricks, wheels, and friendly LEGO people for lots and lots of fun.

Older children build for realism. LEGO Universal Building Sets for children 7–12 have more detailed pieces, like gears, rotors, and treaded tires for more realistic building. One set even has a motor.

LEGO Universal Building Sets will help your children discover something very, very special: themselves.

Universal Building Sets

744

7-12 years old

3-7 years old

LEGO

LEGO club

Special Edition!

LEGO® Friends
FUN AT THE MALL!

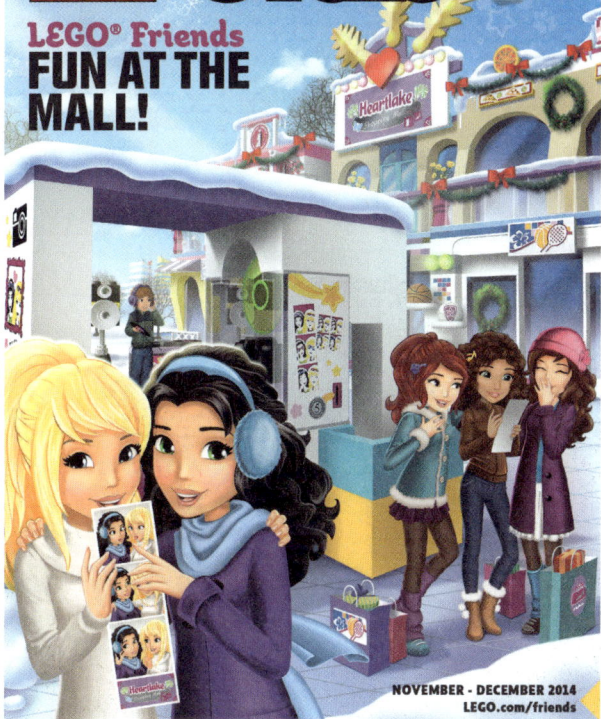

Heartlake

NOVEMBER - DECEMBER 2014
LEGO.com/friends

5th Avenue Mural with Microsoft

S | S███████████M... Jun 3 ↩ ...
to me

Hi Shantell,

I'm an Art Producer at M:United, the Microsoft-focused agency within McCann Erickson — nice to meet you!

The front of the Microsoft store on 5th Avenue in Manhattan is currently boarded up and we're hoping to fill the space with a mural in support of the Black Lives Matter movement. We love your work and would be very excited to partner with you as a Black artist in the New York City community.

Hoping to complete the mural while the protests are still relevant and the boards are still up, ideally no later than this coming Sunday. Would you be interested in and available for this project? Will follow up later this evening with a formal brief to guide the discussion on design and costs.

Q ▽   ⬛

🔴 Liked by **sashmograph** and **thousands of others**

antell_martin Here's an example of what it's like to A) minded of my Blackness, B) how Black pain and pression is commodified with performative allyship, C) at systematic racism looks like within corporations d MOST IMPORTANTLY D) apparently the folks at microsoft and McCann Erickson feel that that the lacklivesmatter Movement and protests will not be evant after this weekend. Education and countability must occur in order to see REAL change. nporting equality only when it's popular is in itself a

AM I NOT A MAN AND A BROTHER

Believe in something. Even if it means sacrificing everything.

Just do it.

Zelensky: 'Being brave is our brand'

Ukrainian

In his nightly address, President Volodymyr Zelensky praised Ukrainia
their courage, which he said should be spread around the world.

"If everyone in the world had at least 10% of the courage we Ukrainia
there would be no danger to international law at all. There would be n
to the freedom of nations. We will spread our courage," he said.

He added that "being brave is our brand", while also calling for the wo
impose bolder sanctions on Russia.

He also said that "the strongest sanction against Russia of all that car
more weapons shipments to use against Russia.

He also commented on news that Russia had been suspended from th
Human Rights Council.

"Russia has long had nothing to do with the concept of human rights.
one day this will change," he said.

"But so far the Russian state and the Russian military are the biggest
the planet to freedom, to human security, to the concept of human rig
such. Obviously."

[f] [y] < Share

Fleeing families tell of Mariupol horror

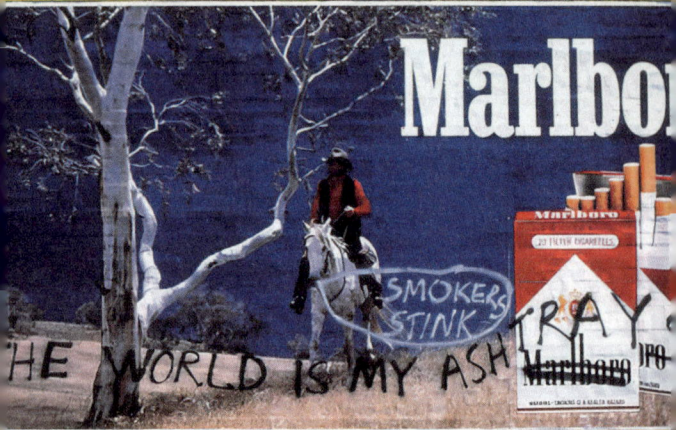

AUSTRALIA URGENTLY
NEEDS MORE

PHANTOM
SPRAYERS

BECAUSE OF GOVERNMENT
ASSISTANCE TO THE
TOBACCO INDUSTRY OUR
FEW PHANTOM SPRAYERS
ARE OVER-WORKED.
  NEW RECRUITS ARE
NEEDED.

PLENTY OF GOOD
TERRITORIES AVAILABLE

START TODAY!

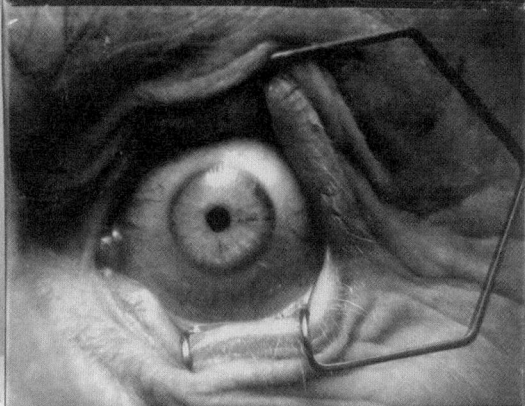

SMOKING CAUSES BLINDNESS

Marlboro Gold

20

BP British Art Displays

Historic
Modern
Contemporary

Supported by BP

bp

FREE ENTRY

BRITAIN
TATE

bp

bp

burning planet
bp

British Pirates

bp beyond poison

bp
blinded by profits

bad

bp
be prepared

bp

bold pollution

bp

WORLD FOR SALE
bad price

bp

bp
bp

bs

p

bpolluted

bp

big problems.

bold pollution

bp

oil.

bp*
biosphere poisoners

bs

bp

bp

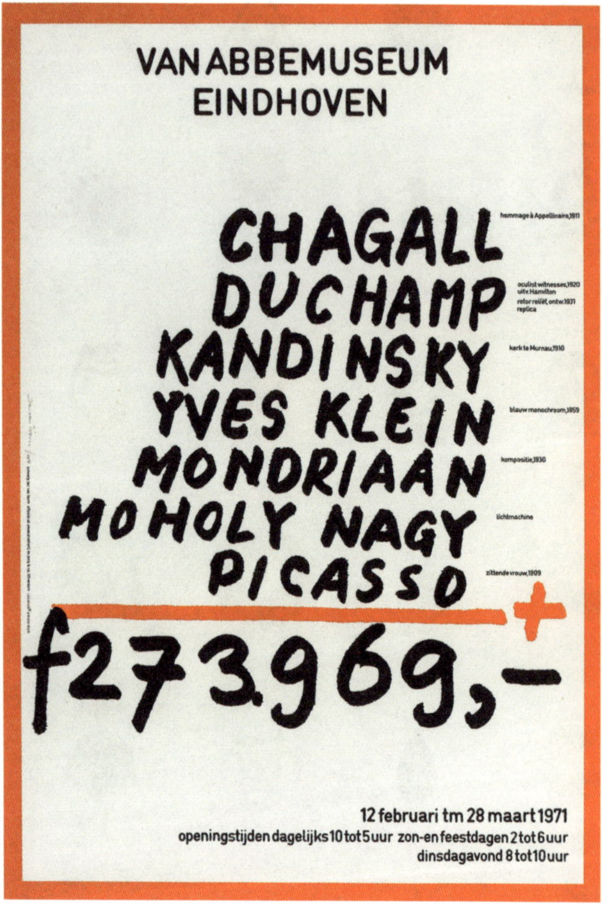

VAN ABBEMUSEUM
EINDHOVEN

CHAGALL   hommage à Apollinaire,1911
DUCHAMP   oculist witnesses,1920
                 uitv. Hamilton
                 rotor reliëf, ontw.1931
                 replica
KANDINSKY   kerk te Murnau,1910
YVES KLEIN   blauw monochroom,1959
MONDRIAAN   kompositie,1930
MOHOLY NAGY   lichtmachine
PICASSO   zittende vrouw,1909

f 273.969,— +

12 februari tm 28 maart 1971
openingstijden dagelijks 10 tot 5 uur   zon-en feestdagen 2 tot 6 uur
dinsdagavond 8 tot 10 uur

VAN ABBEMUSEUM
EINDHOVEN

Marc Chagall
hommage à Apollinaire, 1911

Wassily Kandinsky
kerk te Murnau, 1910

Yves Klein
blauw monochroom, 1959

Marcel Duchamp
roue ro'dè, 1935/1953
replica 1985

Piet Mondriaan
composite, 1930

Laszlo Moholy-Nagy
licht-raum modulator, 1920-22
replica 1970

Pablo Picasso
zittende vrouw, 1909

€ 84.210.000,-

er was eens... de collectie nu
once upon a time... the collection now
doorlopend vanaf november 2013 / ongoing from november 2013

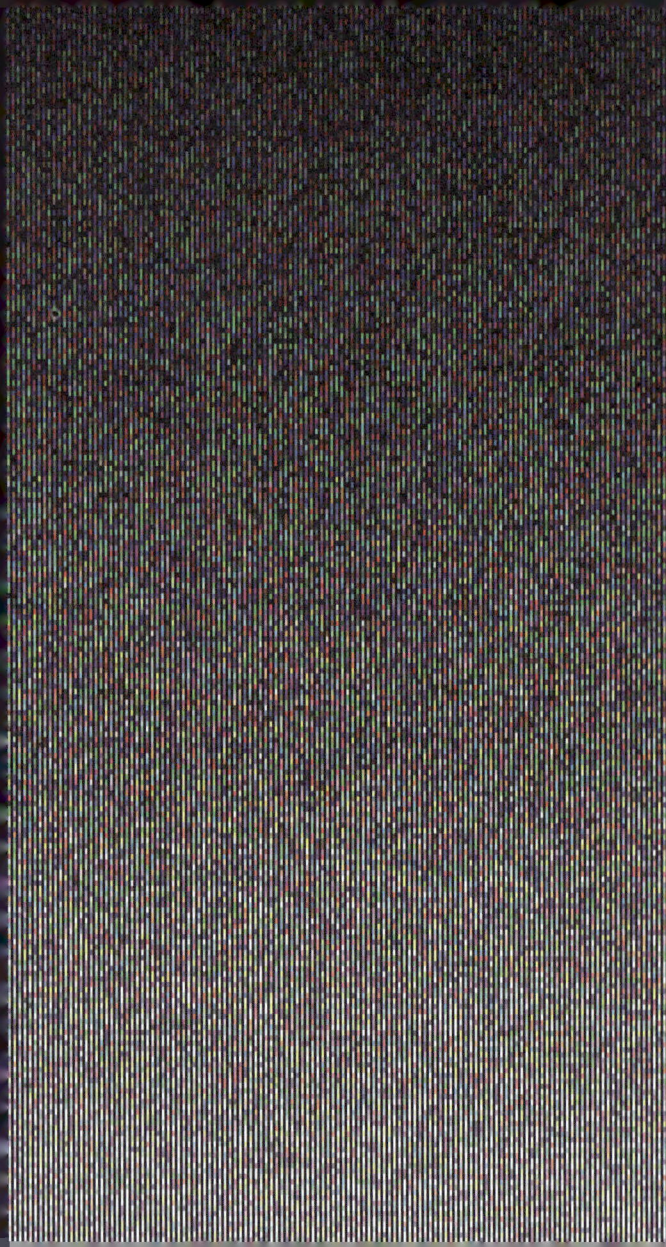

62\63   Mosaic showing bottle of Garum – ancient Roman fish sauce, bearing the inscription *G.F SCOM[bri] SCAURI EX OFFI[ci]NA SCAURI* ('the flower of Scaurus' mackerel garum from the factory of Scaurus'), House of Aulus Umbricus Scaurus, Pompeii. c. 70 A.D. Photo courtesy Dr Sophie Hay.
\
A tin of Lyle's Golden Syrup, first sold in 1885. Claimed to be the world's oldest branded packaging. Photo @TateLyleSugars.

64\65   Record of Transylvanian Cattle-Brand, 1826.
\
Illustration of James Naylor, an English Quaker leader who preached against enclosure and the slave trade. In 1656 Naylor was imprisoned and branded with the letter 'B' for *Blasphemer* on his forehead after he re-enacted Christ's Palm Sunday entry into Jerusalem by entering Bristol on a horse.

66\67   Display of cattle brand markings, Fort Worth, Texas. Photo by Carol M Highsmith.
\
English cigarette card (1928) depicting ancient Egyptian cattle branding – first adopted c. 2700 BCE, as evidenced in hieroglyphics. Collection of The New York Public Library.

68\69   Coin displaying the logo of the Dutch East India Company (Vereenigde Oost-Indische Companie). Conceived in 1602, it is likely the world's first ever multinational company logo, and became a hated symbol of violent colonisation as the Dutch ruthlessly pursued a global spice trade monopoly.
\
Replica of a slave branding iron originally used in the Atlantic slave trade. Displayed at the Museum of Liverpool, England.

70\71   From an engraving by Brantz Mayer, after Francois-Auguste Biard, depicting a slaver as he brands a woman with bound hands, while an attendant holds a lantern, 1854. Originally published in Mayer's book, *Captain Canot or Twenty Years of an African Slaver*.
\
The Branded Hand of Captain Jonathan Walker. Walker was an American abolitionist who was publicly branded on his right hand with the letters "S S" for "slave stealer" after he was caught attempting to help seven men escape slavery. Daguerreotype by Southworth and Hawes, 1845.

72\73   Ancient Roman terracotta oil lamp with makers mark – 'Fortis'. Originating in Northern Italy between AD 70 and AD 230 'factory lamps' bore their manufacturer's mark and were one of the first mass products. Fortis was the most fashionable of all pottery-brands and its products were used until the end of the second century AD.
\
Poster by Peter Behrens for AEG's Metal Filament Bulb, c. 1907. Working for AEG, Behrens is considered history's first industrial designer and the founder of corporate identity, creating logos, advertisements, company publications and architecture with a consistent, unified design.

74\75   Reich Party Congress, Nuremberg, Germany, 1938. Nazi propaganda spectacle photographed by Adolf Hitler's personal photographer, Hugo Jaeger. br.wikipedia.org/wiki/Restr:Kroaz_Gammé.jpg
\
An electronic billboard advertising Coca-Cola in Medford, Massachusetts. One of the products of Coca-Cola's WWII collaboration with the Nazis was the soft drink Fanta. Photo by Yoon S. Byun / The Boston Globe via Getty Images.

76\77   In 1875 the beer company Bass's logo became the first registered trademark.
\
Typographisches Skizzieren und Drucksachenentwerfen, Teil 1: Typoskizze, c. 1936. This official type handbook explains the Nazi regime's acceptable typographic usage along with hand lettering guidelines.

78\79   Soldiers stand at attention in Nuremberg, Germany, listening to a speech by the German Führer, Adolf Hitler during the Nazi Party rally of 1936. Photo Shutterstock.
\
Bottles of Coca-Cola come off the production line. Photo by aapsky.

80\81   Pages from the *Organisationsbuch der NSDAP* (Organizational Handbook of the National Socialist Party), a manual covering many aspects of Nazi public communication and organisation, 1936.
\
Pages from IBM's 'Graphic Design Guide' by Paul Rand, 1981. Images oa.letterformarchive.org

82\83   American cowboy riding a rodeo bull. Photo source unknown.
         \
         Charging Bull bronze sculpture symbolising Wall St in the
         Financial District of New York City. Photo by c_savill.

84\85   Naomi Klein's best-selling book *No Logo*, a groundbreaking
         mix of critique and reportage first published in 2000, and
         subtitled *Taking Aim at the Brand Bullies*.
         \
         In response to *No Logo* The Economist published an industry
         rebuttal with their cover story "Pro Logo: Why Brands Are Good
         for You", in the September 8th, 2001 edition of the magazine.

86\87   Conflict minerals like tin, tantalum, tungsten and gold needed
         for consumer electronics are mined in the Democratic Republic
         of Congo, one of the world's poorest and most unstable
         countries. 60% of cobalt is mined in the DRC and is essential
         for powering rechargeable lithium batteries. Major tech
         companies like Apple, Google, Tesla, Microsoft, and Dell have
         been accused of profiting from child labour in their cobalt
         supply chains. Photo of a child gold miner in Watsa, north-
         eastern Congo, by Marcus Bleasdale, 2004.
         \
         2017 Apple advertising campaign. While Apple has committed
         to developing processes for sourcing minerals from mines
         that benefit Congolese communities, according to a report
         from Global Witness they rely on ITSCI, a certification scheme
         accused of helping "launder" conflict minerals.

88\89   Amazon has aggressively opposed workers unionising in its
         warehouses, with often illegal tactics of intimidation, coercion
         and surveillance. Image of protester at Amazon's Swansea
         fulfilment center in Swansea, Wales, by Matthew Horwood/
         Getty Images, 2018.
         \
         Screenshot from turnerduckworth.com/work/amazon.

90\91   Trader on the floor at the New York Stock Exchange praying
         to his God. Photo by Bryan R. Smith/AFP via Getty Images
         \
         Wally Olins, co founder of Wolff Olins, is known as a pioneer
         of branding consultancy, advocating that branding encom-
         pass the world beyond corporations, such as not-for-profits,
         charities, and nations. Photo famousgraphicdesigners.org/
         wally-olins.

92\93   1985 Amnesty International Stop Torture poster by Stephan Bundi.
\
2008(?) Amnesty International Stop Capital Punishment poster.

94\95   Amnesty International posters by various designers, before
the Wolff Olins global rebrand of 2008.
\
Amnesty International posters post-2008 Wolff Olins' global
rebrand. Various designers.

96\97   Donald Trump launching the Trump Vodka brand in 2007.
Photo WENN / Alamy.
\
Donald Trump signing MAGA hat at campaign rally In Hartford,
Connecticut in 2016. Photo by Matthew Cavanaugh / Stringer.

98\99   Apple's store in Chongqing, China. Photo MacX.
\
@CT_Bergstrom tweet, March 1st 2021.

100\101 Logos automatically generated on designs.ai – an online "A.I.
logo generator and brand builder".
\
Tweet from @Daniel_Sugarman highlighting a bot-generated
app alert from KFC Germany, promoting a menu item as a way
to commemorate Kristallnacht, the 1938 attacks by Nazis on
Jews viewed by many as the start of the Holocaust. The message translates directly as: "Memorial Day of the Reich pogrom
night. Treat yourself easily with more tender cheese with the
crispy chicken. Now at KFCheese!" And the apology an hour
later: "SORRY, A MISTAKE HAPPENED TO US. Due to a mistake
in our system, we have sent an incorrect and inappropriate
message through our App. We regret this a lot, we are going to
immediately check our internal processes, for it to not happen
once again. Please forgive this mistake. Team KFC."

102\103 From The Paul Ekman Group: "The Facial Action Coding System (FACS) is a comprehensive, anatomically based system for
describing all visually discernible facial movement. It breaks
down facial expressions into individual components of muscle
movement, called Action Units (AUs)..." The system is used in
various scientific settings for research, and by animators and
computer scientists interested in facial recognition. paulek-
man.com/facial-action-coding-system.
\

Heat map of City University Website. Screenshot example from user testing eye tracking session. CC BY 2.0, commons. wikimedia.org/wiki/File:Heatmap.jpg, 2010.

104\105 IBM E44123 employee time card for Virginia State University. Photo courtesy Jim Scott.

\
Microsoft Excel spreadsheet for an Australian university academic staff member. Image courtesy anonymous.

106\107 Extracts from article about Flinders University's proposal to close the globally significant Southgate Institute for Health, Society and Equity, and to "dis-establish" the positions of key staff, including the Institute's director, Professor Fran Baum. croakey.org/flinders-university-under-fire-over-shameful-and-stupid-move-against-leading-academics, 2021.

\
Brand guidelines for Flinders University's "Fearless" Campaign by Showpony Advertising, 2021.

108\109 Winston Smith opening a copy of the Newspeak Dictionary in the 1984 film adaption of Orwell's novel *1984*. Directed by Michael Radford and starring John Hurt, Richard Burton, Suzanna Hamilton and Cyril Cusack.

\
"The Airbnb Design Book is a living, modular design manual created to accompany you on your journey". manualcreative. com/work/airbnb.

110\111 Facebook post from Australian fitness guru Kayla Itsines to her 30 million followers. Image Facebook: k.itsines, 2022.

\
Lingerie designed by Jasper Conran on the floor of a looted department store during the 2011 London riots. Photo by Simon Dawson / Bloomberg.

112\113 Branding, like capitalism itself, is predatory, and new markets are relentlessly exploited. This Lego ad from 1981 is well prior to the Friends sub-brand aimed at girls. The sales for 'girls construction toys' tripled in key markets from 2011 to 2014 after Lego's Friends was introduced in 2012.

\
After much criticism of the highly gendered nature of the product and its promotion, Lego launched a campaign in support of International Women's Day 2021, mimicking

the old 'What it is is beautiful' ad for the campaign's 40th anniversary. The highly gendered product remained unchanged. This image shows a 2014 Lego Club magazine cover featuring LEGO Friends having "Fun at the Mall".

114\115 In 2019, Unilever-owned Ben & Jerry's continued its 'brand activism' with the release of a "Justice ReMix'd" ice cream flavour in support of the Black Lives Matter movement. The "limited batch" product raised funds for the Advancement Project National Office, a U.S. national civil rights organisation that works with local grassroots groups on racial justice issues. Photo Ben & Jerry's.
\
Email to U.S. artist Shantell Martin from Microsoft's advertising agency McCann Erickson, and the artist's response, 2020.

116\117 Following the April 4, 1968 assassination of Martin Luther King Jr, the 'Holy Week Uprising' protests and riots flared across the USA. Waves of civil unrest throughout the 1960s triggered by systematic and direct racism were often met by police with excessive and illegal use of force against black citizens. Photo Afro Newspaper / Gado / Getty Images, 1968.
\
A 2017 PepsiCo advertisement shows a festive, multi-racial street protest in which 'model, media personality, and socialite' Kendall Jenner, hands a white police officer a can of Pepsi. After the police officer drinks from the can, the crowd cheers and celebrates. Pepsi canceled the advertisement following accusations of trivialising the Black Lives Matter movement and police violence. PepsiCo, released a statement claiming the ad's purpose was to reach millennials and "to project a global message of unity, peace, and understanding." Image Pepsi Global, via YouTube.

118\119 In 1787 "Potter to the Queen" and Society for the Suppression of the Slave Trade member Josiah Wedgewood, created what some consider to be the first 'activist brand campaign' when he asked one of his company's craftspeople to design the 'supplicant slave' wax seal. The anti-slavery logo was applied to everything from pamphlets and cufflinks to tableware and jewelery, prompting Benjamin Franklin to declare it as "equal to that of the best written Pamphlett." However the pleading, passive pose of the figure and its erasure of enslaved Africans' resistance and struggle, as well as the nature of the image's production and circulation, enforced

the dominant abolitionist narrative as the triumph of white abolitionists. Photo picturinghistory.gc.cuny.edu.
\
The emergence of 'political corporate social responsibility' has seen corporations reinvent themselves as justice-trumpeting activists. Nike's endorsement of American footballer Colin Kaepernick (who initiated kneeling during the U.S. national anthem as a protest against police brutality and racism), reportedly boosted the company's brand value by US$6bn. While calling for racial equality, the Nike campaign is also inevitably framed by the inequality-promoting neoliberal myth of self-made American individualism. Image @Kaepernick7, 2018.

120\121   Russian Prime Minister Vladimir Putin rides a horse during his vacation outside the town of Kyzyl in Southern Siberia on August 3, 2009. Photo Alexsey Druginyn/AFP via Getty Images.
\
BBC News feed. bbc.com/news/live/world-europe-61032786 page/13, Posted at 8:50 8 April 2022.

122\123   McDonald's Siberian franchisee, Russian oil baron Aleksandr Govor, bought the entire Russian business in May 2022, rebranding the fast food chain as Vkusno & tochka ("Tasty and that's it").
\
McDonald's left Russia after more than 30 years and has sold its 847 outlets due to the "humanitarian crisis" and "unpredictable operating environment" caused by the Ukraine war. It has "de-arched" the outlets, removing its name, branding and menu, but retains its trademarks in Russia.

124\125   All manner of radical unifying symbols are now being claimed as branding. (eg. see *Branded Protest* by Ingeborg Bloem & Klaus Kempenaars, BIS). Pussy Riot's balaclavas. Photo dazed-digital.com/artsandculture/article/33090/1/the-pussy-riot-protest-manifesto-nadya-tolokonnikova.
\
Hong Kong pro-democracy protesters' umbrellas are also claimed as branding. Photo Studio Incendo, 2014. CC BY 2.0.

126\127   Brazil's most populous city São Paulo, introduced *Lei Cidade Limpa* (clean city law) in 2006, banning most outdoor advertising, stripping the city of brand propaganda in the public realm. 'Before' photo by Marcelo Palinkas, São Paulo City Council.
\
'After' photo by Marcelo Palinkas, São Paulo City Council.

128\129 Australian Billboard graffiti activists BUGA-UP were founded in 1979 and are one of the world's earliest examples of Culture Jamming, focusing their attention on "tobacco & alcohol promotions and other promotions that were socially and visually assaulting." Photo by BUGA-UP, 1980.
\
BUGA-UP parody ad criticising Australian Government's support of the tobacco industry. Image from *B.U.G.A. U.P. Autumn Catalogue 1980.*

130\131 Australia completely banned tobacco advertising in 1989, and the tobacco industry's decade long legal fight with the country's plain packaging laws were defeated when the final WTO appeals were dismissed in 2020. Image shows fully branded pack of Marlboro Cigarettes, made by Philip Morris, in markets without enforced health warnings, 2018. Photo by Oleg Golovnev / Shutterstock.
\
Australia became the first country in the world to implement plain cigarette packaging in 2012. The legislation's positive health outcomes have inspired many more countries to begin adopting de-branded tobacco packaging. Photo globaltobac-cocontrol.org/tpackss/marlboro-australia-4375.

132\133 BP ended its 26-year sponsorship of the Tate galleries in 2006 after a long campaign by activist group Liberate Tate, who accused the oil company of using Tate to greenwash its image. In the future will there be campaigns directed at public institutions for using corporate branding? Photo Jeffrey Blackler / Alamy, 2010.
\
In the wake of BP's 2010 Deepwater Horizon oil spill in the Gulf of Mexico, critical parodies of the companies logo proliferated. Even simple brand attacks open channels outside the brand's prescription of a "particular ambiance." Various sources.

134\135 Jan van Toorn's 1971 poster for the Van Abbemuseum is a considered expression of the museum's identity, representing both a critique of the art-market, and institutional transparency and public accountability. Collection Van Abbemuseum, Eindhoven, The Netherlands. Photo Peter Cox, Eindhoven, The Netherlands.
\
Jan van Toorn's twin 2013 version of 1971 poster is in dialogue with the original. Collection Van Abbemuseum, Eindhoven, The Netherlands. Photo Peter Cox, Eindhoven, The Netherlands.

Following is a substitute brand manual introducing the three dimensions of post-branding as an alternative branding framework. Here is a plan for the ethical communication of collective identity liberated from a totalising, predatory ideology.

03.

MANUAL

03. pg 146

CONTENTS

1.
transparency
& open source
principles

TRANSPARENCY ✓

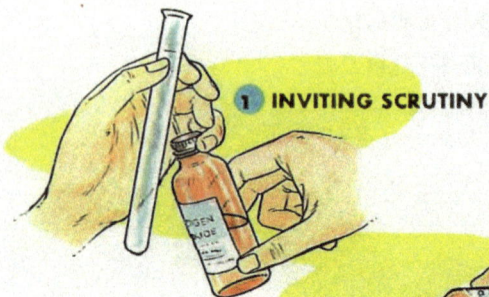

1 INVITING SCRUTINY

TOWARDS 2

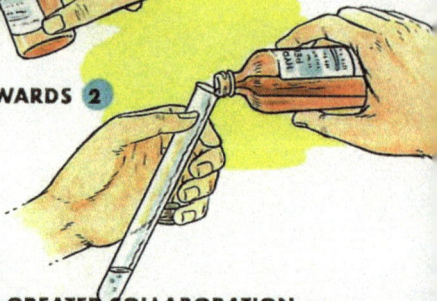

3 GREATER COLLABORATION

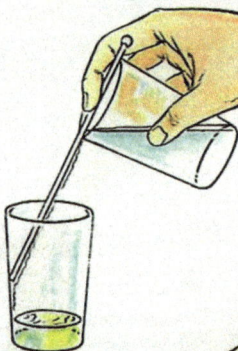

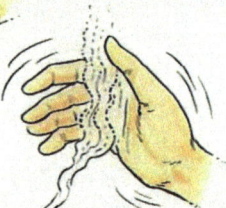

4 AND TRUST.

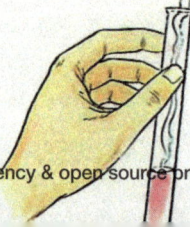

Suspicion,

defensive

'hiding

away',

isolation,

surveillance.

Openness

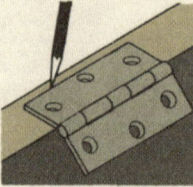

1. Breaking down

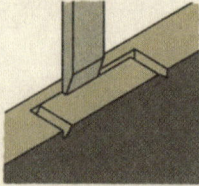

2. hierarchies.

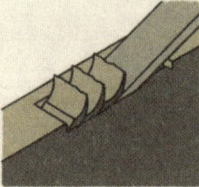

3. Fostering

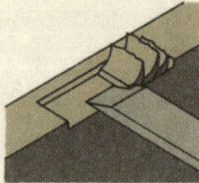

4. alternatives.

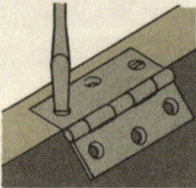

5. Trusting people

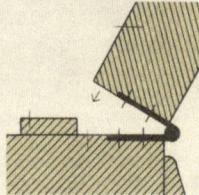

6. to act.

CONTROL

X

1. Imposing rigid boundaries

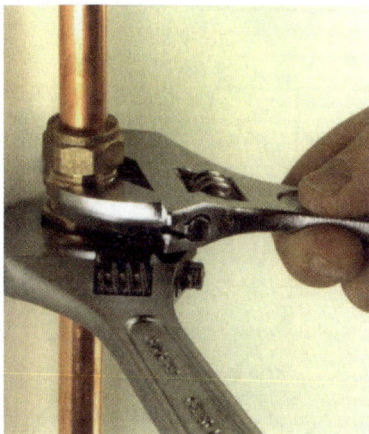

2. Enforcing proprietary domination

REVELATION

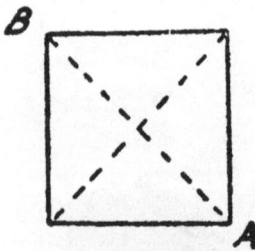

1. Exposing

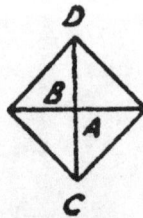

2. reality.

3. Asking

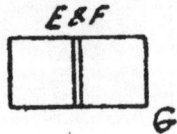

4. what

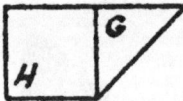

5. new

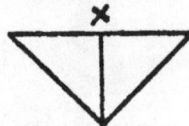

6. realities

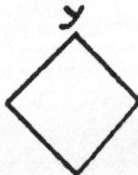

7. might be

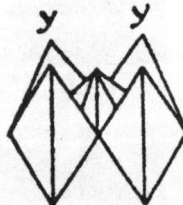

8. possible.

Distortion

1. Deliberate

2. or

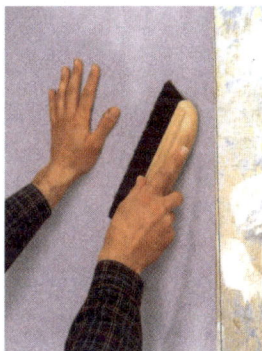

3. casual

4. deception.

2.
participatory
design
approaches

Participation

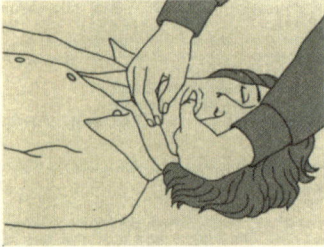

Including stakeholders

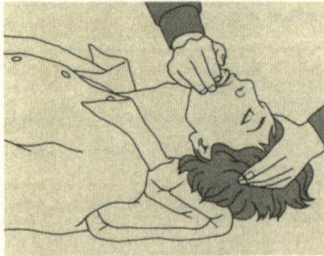

in decisions

that impact them.

EXCLUSION

Fig. 1. LIMITING AND

Fig. 2. GUARDING PROCESS

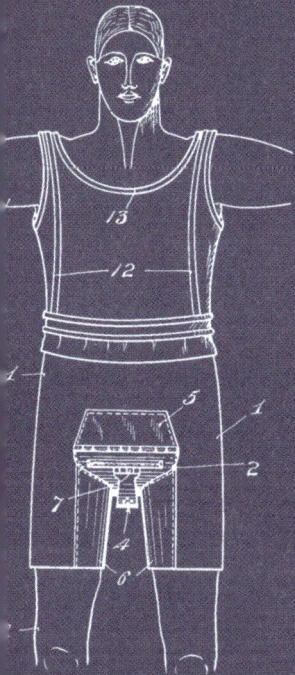

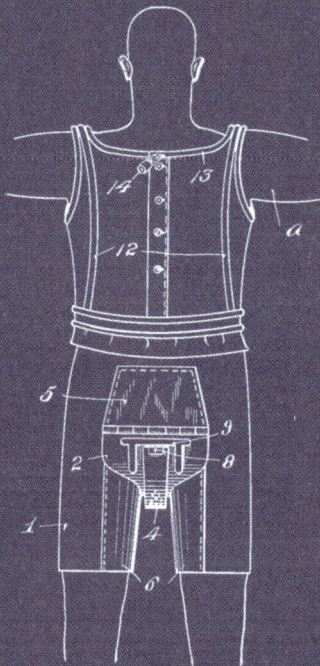

Collaboration

Trust.

Connection.

Solidarity.

X

Competition

1. Suspicion.

2. Division.

3. Opposition.

SOCIAL ENGAGEMENT

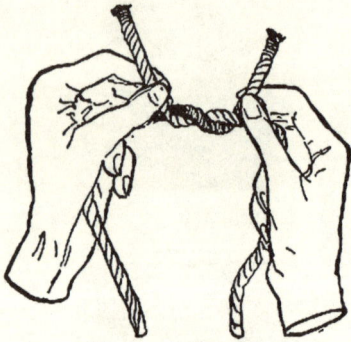

A. Relations

B. that benefit society

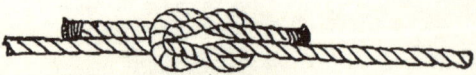

C. and the environment.

Consumption:

☐ **Passive**

☐ **consumerism.**

3.
diversity
& commoning

Cohesion

1 Meaningfully connected.

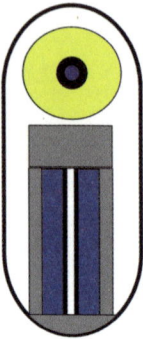

2 Consistency based

3 on respect

4 for diversity.

Homogeneity

Sameness.

No room for

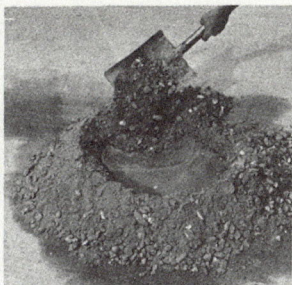

creativity

or diversity.

DIALOGUE

Fig. 9 — Creating space for

Fig. 10 — real conversations,

Fig. 11 — Including criticism

Fig. 12 — and disagreement.

JAK

X

a) Promoting

b) or **c)** selling.

Criticality and Imagination

Questioning status quo.

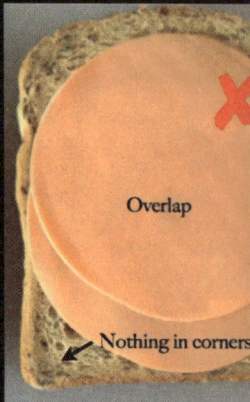

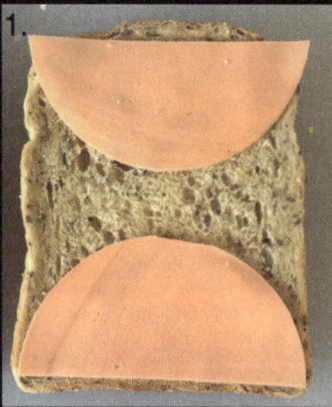

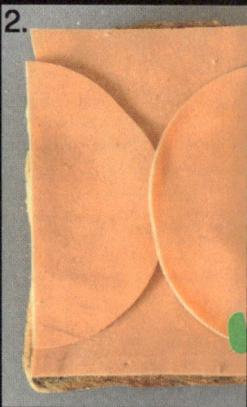

Overlap

Nothing in corners

1.

2.

Commodification

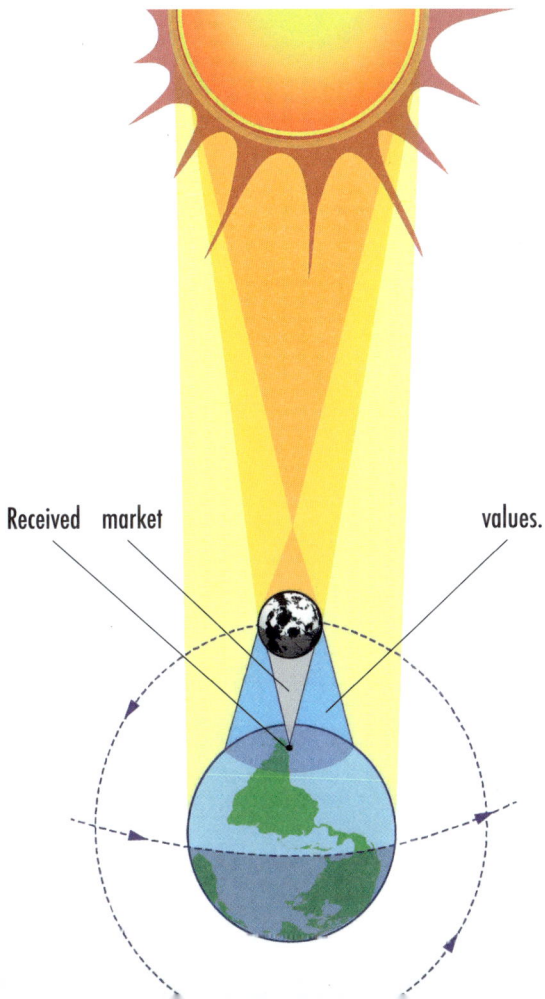

Received market values.

Original image sources: 152 – *The Golden Book of Chemistry Experiments* by Robert Brent and illustrated by Harry Lazarus, Golden Press, USA, 1960. 153 – *The Readers Digest Do-it-yourself Manual*, Readers Digest, Aus, 1972. 154 – *The Readers Digest Do-it-yourself Manual*, Readers Digest, Aus, 1972. 155 – *The Readers Digest Do-it-yourself Manual*, Readers Digest, UK, 2004. 156 – *Winter Nights Entertainments* by R.M. Abraham, Dover Publications, USA, 1932. 157 – *The Readers Digest Do-it-yourself Manual*, Readers Digest, UK, 2004. 160 – *The Readers Digest Do-it-yourself Manual*, Readers Digest, Aus, 1972. 161 – *US Patent No. 875845, Sexual Armor* by Ellen E Perkins, 1908. 162 – *Breakdance* by William H Watkins & Eric N Franklin, Contemporary Books, USA, 1984. 163 – *Self Defense and Physical Fitness* by Antonino Rocca, Pocket Books, UK, 1965. 164 – *Reef Knot*, source unknown. 165 – *McDonald's Training Station Observation Checklist*, 2014. 168 *Ablation mechanism firing sequence*, en.wikipedia.org/wiki/ Thermonuclear_weapon, CC BY-SA 2.5, 2006. 169 – *The Readers Digest Do-it-yourself Manual*, Readers Digest, Aus, 1972. 170 – *The Manual of Judo* by E J Harrison 4th Dan, W Foulsham & Co, UK, 1952. 171 – *Learn to Ride* by Ella Winblad Von Walter, Barron's Educational Series, US, 1976. 172 – *Good Sandwich Guide*, source unknown. 173 – *Geometry of a Total Solar Eclipse*, eclipse2017.nasa.gov/eclipse-101, NASA, 2017.

A.
applications

This is the fun bit at the end of corporate brand manuals where we get to see applied examples illustrating the viability of the system.

Our proposal for a post-branding alternative is presented as a broad framework. We also want to show that post-branding practice already exists, and while branding is by far the dominant way of engaging with the world when designing identities, a practical alternative is available.

We should be aware that branding is naturalised and, as an ideology, needs us to believe that no alternative is possible. Positioning a contested matter as above political contest is always an unassailable political ploy.

We also need to be aware that as the dominant logic, branding and its evangelists will try to hinder the rise of an alternative (most commonly by claiming that branding's critics overstate its power, and therefore its ability to cause harm, while simultaneously spruiking its transformative power to clients). Even though post-branding is in this way a critical, alternative and oppositional practice, it is offered here as a general foundation.

Post-branding is 'practical theory' and like all good theories, it is exploratory and questioning. It is not intended as a final answer to the problem of branding, rather a pathway to new possibilities.

The real work is yet to be done in studios and agencies, in classrooms and communities. Many of the proposed post-branding principles have already been expressed in real applications. The ideas themselves are not new, but using them to replace branding's exploitative and predatory principles can be radical.

The following projects demonstrate diverse examples of nuanced post-branding approaches. Although this book critiques branding as a broad phenomenon, it also focuses on identity design as a key dimension of branding relevant to visual communicators.

In opposition to branding, post-branding aims to avoid producing extractive relations. At the start of every post-branding project is an evaluation about who we are working with. While professional designers can apply post-branding in their practice – supporting organisations working across different sectors in society – post-branding, by definition, can't be done for clients and causes that harm our world.

An assessment of the different dimensions of the project's causes and/or client is always necessary. The nature of such an assessment is interdisciplinary and needs to connect design with knowledge from other realms, such as humanities and social sciences.

Not every strategic principle can be applied to every project. Nor are these the only strategies that can counter branding's harm. The complexities inherent to each post-branding project needs case by case consideration. Post-branding demands honest and thorough attention aligned to concrete ethical principles and deep knowledge about how design works in the world.

Because post-branding sees the public sphere as inherently open, participatory and democratic, our role as designers is to guard these principles through our work. Designing identities is seen as a collective articulation of issues, needs and futures, and our work needs to focus on building these emancipatory alternative worlds.

EXTINCTION

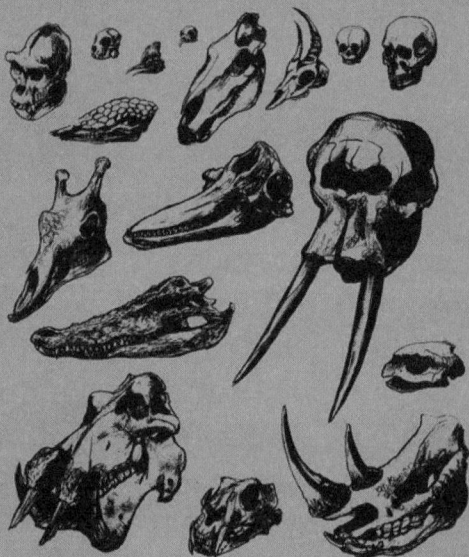

EVERYONE GONE FOREVE

extinction
rebellion

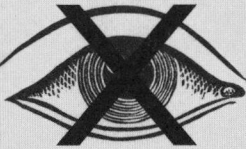

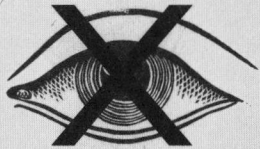

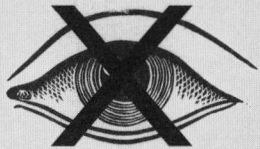

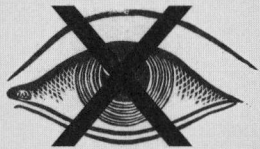

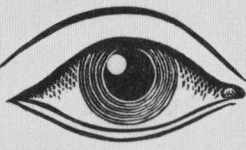

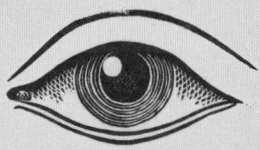

extinction
rebellion

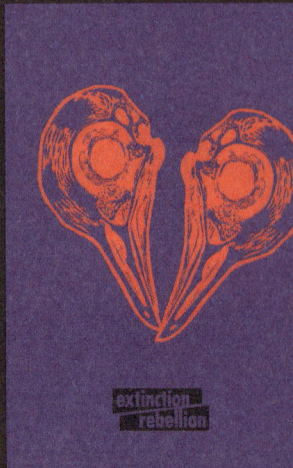

MORE DESIGN TOOLS. START BY USING THESE. THEN ADD MORE OF YOUR OWN. AND PLEASE SHARE THEM BACK.

The XR wood blocks and illustrations allow us to communicate the climate and ecological crisis in a unique way. Sometimes bleak, often humourous, always unmistakably XR.

Use them however you like – there are plenty of usage examples in the artwork downloads – and add to them!

Share your own creations at xrdesigngroup@gmail.com

EXTINCTION REBELLION IS STRICTLY NON-COMMERCIAL.

The design assets in this guide are distributed on a strictly non-commercial basis. *And there are two absolute usage conditions.*

1/ The Extinction Symbol may *never* be used for (or associated with) any commercial purposes – even fundraising. This is a non-negotiable rule and there are no exceptions.

The symbol is not ours. It was created in 2011 by street artist ESP, and is loaned to us in good faith.

2/ There is no Extinction Rebellion commercial merchandise. Feel free to make your own XR clothes, posters, art etc – *but give them away*. Remember, we're in the business of overturning business-as-usual.

You may use XR design assets (but never the Extinction Symbol) for the promotion of XR fundraising activites.

Extinction Rebellion uses non-violent, disruptive civil
disobedience to overcome the limitations of established
forms of protest. The decentralised, international and
politically non-partisan movement aims to persuade
governments and businesses to act justly on the Climate
and Ecological Emergency.

Clive Russell, a designer at XR and This Ain't Rock'n'Roll
notes: "XR is a do-it-together movement. All our design
and artwork can be used non-commercially for the purpose
of planet saving."

Part of making the organisation inclusive and accessible
has been the free availability of their protest graphics to
download from their website. Not guarding and hiding
communication processes and outputs has allowed people
to take a sense of ownership over the rebellion, while
encouraging the making of their own protest materials.
It also helps inspire a public sense of collective
responsibility.

Russell says: "Transparent and freely available design
processes allow anyone to express themselves within
a consistent framework. How do you express yourself
differently within a society that values material wealth over
everything else? You give your work away for free. It really
is that simple – if more people worked freely more often
(with a network of like-minds to support it) we'd quickly
shift into different ways of valuing ourselves and one
another – *Production and Consumption* becomes *Care
and Freedom*, to paraphrase the late great David Graeber."

1.2 Openness not control

Burst Open by Inkahoots

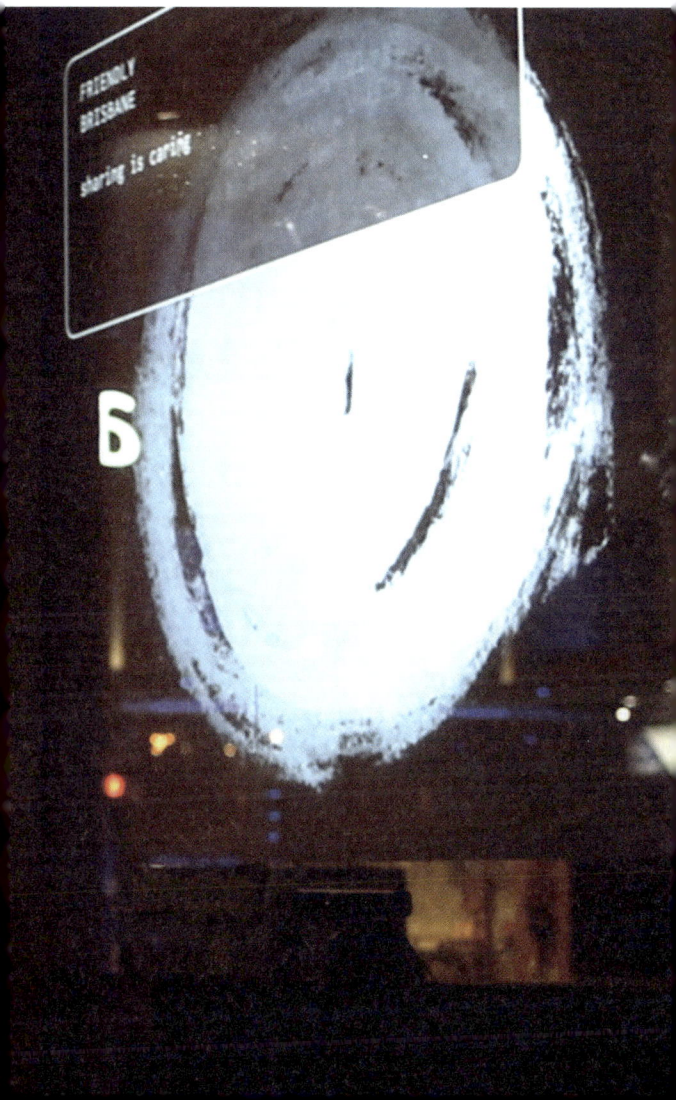

ific Design Library Brisbane

ralised design mod-
e ability to enable
ncing diversity,
creases innovation,
ness and design
s

Ben Henley. Brisbane

Culture is an open system.
A chaotic, non-linear,
aperiodic mess. Culture is
a remix. Open source is
a promise, rather than a
product.

Jonathan Nalder. San Diego

The chance for beginners to
use the shoulders of giants
that have gone before as
the platform to make their
own leap from

Jo. Wellington

If Newton was standing on
the shoulders of giants, open
source allows us to balance
a giant crane on top, with a
whole heap of beanstalks on
top of that. Design reaches
higher as a result.

Cathy Po

Freedom
towards
destiny.

gle. Sydney

That means Freedom,
o means "Free". You
al something that is
borrow it, bend it
ose it. It's a historical
hat should not be
ed".

10

Mike Bogle. Sydney

Access. That means Freedom,
which also means "Free". You
can't steal something that is
free. You can borrow it, bend it
& re-purpose it. It's a historical
process that should not be
"monetized".

11

Mike Bogle. Sydney

Access. That means Freedom,
which also means "Free". You
can't steal something that is
free. You can borrow it, bend it
& re-purpose it. It's a historical
process that should not be
"monetized".

12

Nick Phillips. Brighton

No rights reserved. All wrongs
righted.

13

**Christian
Melbourn**

Greater e
comes th
and prog
tioning ce
client / us

. Brisbane

e great people who
e your ideas even
d who help spread
n, influence and
nuch faster and wider
single person could
ir own

18

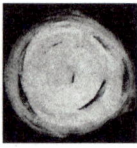

Friendly. Brisbane

Sharing is caring.

19

Ilka Blue. Brisbane

Shifting the paradigm into an
ecological age, where people
are connected by sharing
skills rather than separated by
owning them.

20

Sheena Marcus. Portland

Creative communism.

21

James W

for every
everyone

cguire. Brisbane

e sun for long
can attract all kinds
ms, some intent on

26

Marcus D. Perth

An antidote to the posses-
sive, suspicious, greedy,
grasping of capitalism.

27

Alina Marsi. New York

From each according to our
ability, to each according to
our need.

28

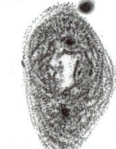

**Communication Design
Federation University.
Ballarat**

contributing to rather than

29

**Commun
Federatic
Ballarat**

contribut

an exhibition exploring
the emerging, global open
source design movement

4 October - 24 December
Gallery Artisan
381 Brunswick Street
Fortitude Valley
Brisbane Australia

BURST
OPEN

artisan   architecture   Inkahoots   nimamaine

BEN HENLEY
BRISBANE

Culture is an open system. A chaotic, non-linear, aperiodic mess. Culture is a remix. Open source is a promise, rather than a product.

To create an identity for Burst Open, an exhibition about open source design, Inkahoots invited creative submissions from around the world.

The logo and a morphing animation ('Open Morph') was assembled with contributor's submissions. The interactive animation was then projected in the gallery's street-front window and controlled by engaged pedestrians' body gestures.

By rotating arms and tracing the figure of an 'O' in the air, the submitted 'O' images morphed forwards or backwards and could be paused by raising arms, displaying the contributors' supplied name, location, and statement about open source design. The posture with which participants begin tracing the arc of the 'O' to trigger the projected animation is also the semaphore symbol for 'O'.

The process invited participation and critical contributions at key stages of the project's creation and implementation. Burst Open was the first performative, augmented, open source exhibition identity – demonstrating that open source is a viable and exciting opportunity for inclusive identity development.

As one contributor's submission put it – open source is: "where people are connected by sharing skills rather than separated by owning them."

1.3 Revelation not distortion

Wings of Paradise by Greenpeace

How can the tragedy of rainforest destruction be revealed
without disengaging an audience?

Greenpeace contributor Alexander Navarro writes: "For
too long the story of Indonesian forests has been painted
with the darkness of burning rainforests, disappearing
species and displaced communities. After ravaging the
forests of Borneo and Sumatra, the palm oil industry has
reached the final frontier, Papua, home to these Birds
of Paradise. Both the birds and the forest could be lost
if we allow these companies to continue."

The Greenpeace initiated Wings of Paradise project
has grown into a global movement with street artists and
volunteers from Melbourne to Taipei, Vienna to Tokyo –
linking remote threatened forests to urban communities of
care. The movement helps counter the palm oil industry's
concocted "sustainable" certifications, deceptive labeling,
evidence-free advertising, vague and misleading research,
and other attempts at greenwashing.

For project curator Rosie Strickland the interventions are:
"connecting iconic urban landscapes with the struggle to
turn the tide on deforestation and species extinction. The
Birds of Paradise: displaced from their forest home into
the urban environment, appeared as a messenger-symbol
of the need to protect their home from deforestation."

2.1 Participation not Exclusion

un VOYAG

Nuit Debout by Sébastien Marchal

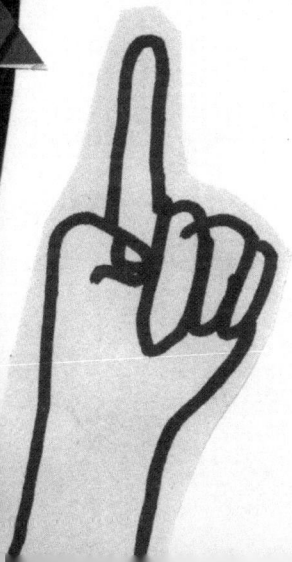

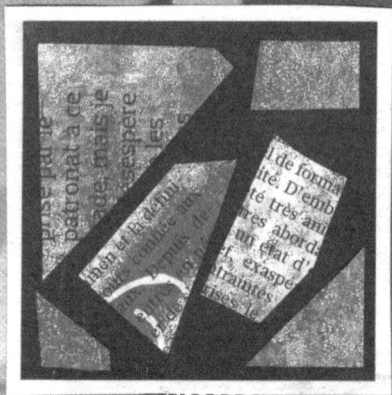

Faire sauter les verrous

NUIT DEBOUT

RÉSISTER

NUIT DEBOUT

DÉSirlusiON

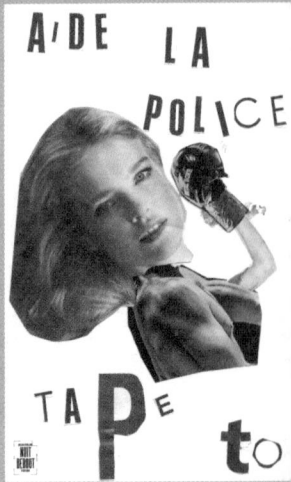

AiDE LA POLICE

TAPE to

SERIAL POLITICOS
fabriqué des monstres

système

SNIF !

In 2016 France's student groups and unions organised
a series of large-scale street protests in opposition to
proposed labor market liberalisation and President
François Hollande's government more generally. Initially
occupying the Place de la République, the Nuit debout
protests rapidly spread to over 30 cities across France
and then to many others around the world. Marchal's
poster workshops with protesters at the occupation site
mirrored the democratic imperatives of the assemblée
générale.

Opening up the design process to movement members
themselves has many advantages including encouraging
ownership of outcomes, boosting confidence and resilience,
helping strengthen relationships, and uncovering real needs
and interests beyond the potentially limited assumptions
of established designers and organisers.

Marchal says: "I helped people who wanted to participate
to create, with markers, scissors, glue, magazines and
newspapers, on A4 formats. Then I scanned and adjusted
the results, put them in black and white, and printed
them in big and cheap B&W format that were pasted up
at the site or given to groups who used them to replace
advertisements around the city."

Marchal also introduced his typeface *Commune* to
the protesters – a 240 version font family he originally
designed during his post-graduate study at ESAD Amiens.
In support of the movement's communication he gave the
fonts away under a creative commons license so that they
could be freely used by protesters during the occupation
and beyond.

2.2 Collaboration not Competition

COMMITTEE

THE SPECIES IN WHICH PEACE AND MU

SOCIABLE SPECIES DECAY.

Justseeds Open Type Project

"HE NEEDS, TASTES, ASPIRATIONS & INTERESTS
F MANKIND ARE NEITHER SIMILAR NOR NATURALLY
ARMONIOUS; OFTEN THEY ARE DIAMETRICALLY OPPOSED
ND ANTAGONISTIC. ON THE OTHER HAND, THE LIFE OF
ACH INDIVIDUAL IS SO CONDITIONED BY THE LIFE OF
THERS THAT IT WOULD BE IMPOSSIBLE, EVEN ASSUMING
 WERE CONVENIENT TO DO SO, TO ISOLATE ONESELF
ND LIVE ONE'S OWN LIFE. SOCIAL SOLIDARITY IS A FACT
ROM WHICH NO ONE CAN ESCAPE."

-ERRICO MALATESTA

HE WORDS AROUND THE GRAPHIC BY PYOTR KROPOTKIN

BCDEFGHIJKLMNOPQRSTUVWXYZO123
567890!@#$%^&*().,<>?/-AÀÁÂÄÃÇÈÉ
ËÌÍÎÏÑÒÓÔÖÕØÙÚÛÜ

**BCDEFGHIJKLMNOPQRSTUVWXYZO123
567890!@#$%^&*().,<>?/-AÀÁÂÄÃÈÉÊ
ÌÍÎÏÑÒÓÔÖÕØÙÚÛÜ**

BCDEFGHIJKLMNOPQRSTUVWXYZO123
567890!#$%^&().,?/-AÀÁÂÄÇÈÉ
ËÌÍÎÏÑÒÓÔÖØÕÙÚÛÜ

**TYPE-FACE BASED ON THE SHAPES
ADE WHEN CUTTING LETTERS IN RELIEF.**
'AILABLE IN THREE VARIATION 'LIGHT

ABORTION ON DEMAND FREE SAFE LEGAL

HOUGH THE ASSOCIATION
ANTI-FASCIST WOMEN'S
RIENTATION WAS COMMUNIST,
S GOAL WAS TO UNITE
HE LARGEST POSSIBLE
UMBER OF WOMEN, WITHOUT
ISTINGUISHING BETWEEN
DEOLOGIES, TO JOIN FORCES IN
HE FIGHT AGAINST FASCISM.

BILBAO

ABCDE

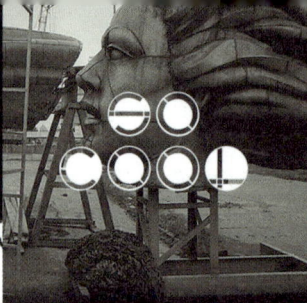

SO COOL

SO GRACI

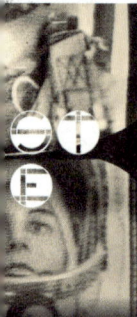

CT T E

DUCT

UNC VEI CE

VED IN A BLANKET OF MIST

TH WAV

S AR

I WAIT

ON SILENC

Justseeds is a worker-owned art and design activist co-operative spanning the U.S., Canada, and Mexico. Their Justseeds Open Type Project creates open-access fonts for use by activists. Members collaborate to release freely distributed font collections designed by themselves or based on historical references. Their 'Antifascistas Font Packs' are drawn from letterforms found in Spanish civil war era revolutionary feminist, communist and anarchist organisation publications.

Coop artist Alec Dunn recalls a collaborative process: "[fellow coop members] Josh and Joy were both swamped with projects so I built Joy's *Medicine* and Josh's *Anarchist Encyclopedia* fonts from relatively small samples with their feedback. I enjoy the process of attempting to decipher the fonts' patterns and structures, of trying to parse how letters can be constructed in a particular style."

Regarding the historically derived fonts, Dunn believes that: "if your values align with the sources, most of the original designers would be happy to see their work carry forward into new movements. A nice example is the typeface I adapted from the masthead of the publication *Mujeres Libres* (anarcho-feminist journal) repurposed in Sarah Farahat's print made in solidarity with the women of Iran. There's an interesting historical collaboration there, an idea imbued in a font that is being carried forward."

Right to the City by image-shift

image-shift's *right to the city* campaign manifests a unique, sustained engagement with the designer's own neighborhood of Kottbusser Tor in Berlin's Kreuzberg.

The project is a collaboration with the local tenant initiative, Kotti & Co, struggling against rising social housing rents. Communication for a diverse range of protest activities such as demonstrations, concerts, reading sessions, discussion rounds, parties etc. have been developed and designed by image-shift. This includes humorously quoting and redirecting tourism artifacts like postcards and Milton Glaser's I♥NY logo, as well as facilitating community members' own creative contributions.

image-shift's Sandy Kaltenborn says: "besides being a tenant initiative, it is a project of diversity – bringing together a very wide range of different people, who would usually live a typical urban life next to each other but not connecting with each other". This rich form of community participation is successfully resisting a disempowering culture of consumptive gentrification. Since 2010 the struggle has achieved significant victories, such as a rentstop for all Berlin social housing flats, the remunicipalisation of the privatised social housing flats in Kreuzberg and beyond, and a Berlin wide referendum to democratize communal housing companies. The referendum on the expropriation of profit/stock market-run big housing companies also started at Kottbusser Tor.

Ayushman Bharat by Lopez Design

ପ୍ରାଥମିକ ସ୍ୱାସ୍ଥ୍ୟ କେନ୍ଦ୍ର
ଅଜନଗର

Reaching out to a billion-plus people across 650,244 villages and over 300 cities, officially speaking 22 languages and 1652 dialects, New Delhi-based Lopez Design created an identity with a dynamic common visual and conceptual foundation for 150,000 community health centres across India.

Rather than ignoring and flattening cultural difference, the Ayushman Bharat identity visually celebrates diversity, without limiting identification and recognition.

The centres deliver universal and free comprehensive primary health care to some of India's poorest rural communities. The flexible yet modular identity enables the expression of unique regional character for each site, its implementation employing local craftspeople and promoting indigenous crafts. Each centre is painted with locally specific cultural motifs, chosen by the community and rendered on facades around prominent architectural features, reinforcing the buildings themselves as one of the program's main communication mediums.

The design demonstrates how even agencies with a conventional corporate design focus can create solutions that promote recognition with diversity while resisting branding's compulsive regimented cultural and visual standardisations.

3.2 Dialogue not Publicity

THE
MUSEUM
OF
FAILURES

The Museum of Failures by Disnovation.org

INVENTORS KILLED BY THEIR OWN INVENTIONS

List of inventors killed by their own inventions

Automotive

→ Sylvester H. Roper, inventor of the eponymous steam-powered bicycle, died of a heart attack or subsequent crash during a public speed trial in 1896. It is unknown whether the crash caused the heart attack or the heart attack caused the crash.

→ William Nelson (c. 1879–1903), a General Electric employee, invented a new way to motorize bicycles. He then fell off his prototype bike during a test run.

→ Francis Edgar Stanley (1849–1918) was killed while driving a Stanley Steamer automobile. He drove his car into a woodpile while attempting to avoid farm wagons travelling side by side on the road.

Aviation

→ Ismail ibn Hammad al-Jawhari (died c. 1003–1010), a Kazakh-Turkic scholar from Farab, attempted to fly using two wooden wings and a rope. He leapt from the roof of a mosque in Nishapur and fell to his death.

→ Jean-François Pilâtre de Rozier was the first known fatality in an air crash when his Rozière balloon crashed on 15 June 1785 while he and Pierre Romain attempted to cross the English Channel.

Marie Skłodowska-Curie (1867–1934) invented the process to isolate radium after co-discovering the radioactive elements radium and polonium. She died of aplastic anemia as a result of prolonged exposure to ionizing radiation emanating from her research materials. The dangers of radiation were not well understood at the time.

First actual case of bug being found (9 September 1945).

THE FIRST COMPUTER BUG

Museum of Bug

The First Computer Bug Moth found trapped between points at Relay # 70, Panel F, of the Mark II Aiken Relay Calculator while it was being tested at Harvard University, 9 September 1945. The operators affixed the moth to the computer log, with the entry, "First actual case of bug being found." They put out the word that they had debugged the machine, thus introducing the term debugging a computer program. In 1988, the log, with the moth still taped to the entry, was in the Naval Surface Warfare Center Computer Museum at Dahlgren, Virginia.

A software bug is an error, failure or fault in a computer program or system that causes it to produce an incorrect or unexpected result, or to behave in unintended ways. The process of fixing bugs is termed "debugging" and often uses formal techniques or tools to pinpoint bugs, and since the 1950s, some computer systems have been designed to also deter, detect or auto-correct various computer bugs during operations.

Most bugs arise from mistakes and errors made in either a program's source code or its design, or in components and operating systems used by such programs. A few are caused by compilers producing incorrect code. A program that contains a large number of bugs, and bugs that seriously interfere with its functionality, is said to be buggy (defective). Bugs can trigger errors that may have ripple effects. Bugs may have subtle effects or cause the program to crash or enter.

TAY (CHATTER BOT)

Artificial Intelligence Failures

On Wednesday (Mar. 23, 2016), Microsoft unveiled a friendly AI chatbot named Tay that was modeled to sound like a typical teenage girl. The bot was designed to learn by talking with real people on Twitter and the messaging apps Kik and GroupMe. ("The more you talk the smarter Tay gets," says the bot's Twitter profile.) But the well-intentioned experiment quickly descended into chaos, racial epithets, and Nazi rhetoric.

Tay started out by asserting that "humans are super cool." But after less than a

MUSEUM OF FAILURES
FLOOR -4 | ROOM 11
INVENTORS KILLED
BY THEIR OWN INVENTIONS

the
MUSEUM of Failures

Disnovation.org have conceived The Museum of Failures as a "contributive museum", dedicated to the dark and underrepresented narratives about technology. They write: "Progress, innovation and linear growth are cornerstones of our contemporary economies, social systems, even personal faith and belief. The very prevalence of these models and values requires that we unearth, create and circulate alternative, counter-narrative and parallel accounts."

As well as designed artifacts, performances, and database installations inviting public dialogue, the group stage workshops from which they compile and produce a printed publication, and are creating an online, participatory repository for statements, artifacts, anecdotes, documents, essays and case studies. They state: "Technological development is often recounted as the exploitation and instrumentalisation of heroic moments and individuals, ignoring the long shadow of aborted projects, flops, errors, malfunctions, ethical disavowals and disasters."

Branders now do talk about dialogue, but they don't really mean *dialogue*, where there is mutual opportunity for open disagreement. They refer rather to 'conversational marketing' where mutable digital technologies enable 'agile sprints', with 'constant feedback loops' and the delivery of 'personalised consumer engagements', all towards endless extractive commercial potential.

WWMII Inc. by LOKI

WW(W)MJJ
inc.

WHITE MEAT

LANCEMENT DE DISQUE
AUTO-CANNIBALISM

AVEC

1,000,000 CUTS
EMPTY BELLY

L.A.J.B. / VENDREDI 9 OCTOBRE 2015 / 20H / 8$
WWW.WWMIIINC.COM

AVEC INVITÉS SPÉCIAUX

Lady Heavy · THE McGILL GHETTO SMOOTH JAZZ ENSEMBLE

L.A.J.B. / MERCREDI 7 OCTOBRE 2015 / 20H / 8$

WWW.WWMIIINC.COM

World (War) Music International Incorporated Inc. (2015) was a satirical branding campaign for a fictional record label. The project was initiated by the Artivistic collective (an all-POC art and research collective) and commissioned by the performance art festival VIVA Art Action.

A series of posters, a promotional music video and website were created for a roster of fake bands on the fictional label, whose names (*Identity Politikss*, *White Meat*, *Auto-Cannibalism*, *1,000,000 Cuts*, etc.) and performances present a humorous critique of the whiteness and classism of the local art and independent music scene, and the systemic racism of the white liberal (Canadian) state more broadly. The designs hijacked a commission to promote the festival with an independent agenda, while still pointing their audience towards the festival.

LOKI designer Kevin Yuen Kit Lo writes: "The design and imagery subverted vested cultural tropes and commodity forms (the music video) while also genuinely celebrating the politics and joy of existing and resisting from a position of difference and diasporic identity. The campaign hijacked a commercial design commission to promote the VIVA festival with our own agenda as a furtive project, a creative form of institutional critique, playfully biting the hand that feeds."

Following is an appendix of discussions, arguments and quizzes as supplementary post-branding background.

04.

pg 234

CONTEXT

Pre-Post-Branding
A Conversation with Brian Holmes & Oliver Vodeb

Looking back at our long journey in the counterculture of communication, the early 2000s were some of the most exciting times. The rich culture of media activism and critical intellectualism in Europe was on fire, profoundly shaping how we think about communication. The ideas and practices developed during this period have circulated globally but have penetrated disciplines of knowledge differently. Media and communication disciplines widely debated the emerging capabilities of networked communication, tactical media and the wider socio-cultural changes which enabled the emergence of new radical communication practices. The discipline of design however remained largely closed and unresponsive, the critical discussions happening mostly on the radical margins. One such exception was the Memefest International Festival of Radical Communication, an initiative I co-founded, which in 2002 focused on the investigations of alternative epistemologies, critique of and counter strategies to branding. Two decades later, the ideas and critiques in the following 2003 conversation resonate optimistically again.

Jason Grant and I wrote a post-branding critique, which you can read in this book. In 2016 Jason published an essay for the U.S. design blog Design Observer, titled 'Against Branding', based on talks he gave at the Asia Pacific Design Library's lecture series, and then in 2020, not long after we evolved the ideas in a small Brisbane zine, Jason's design studio Inkahoots and myself developed for Greenpeace International (an attempt at) the first commissioned post-branding design project. And so it goes, while ideas take time to evolve and manifest in practice, it might well be, to paraphrase Victor Hugo, that the time for post-branding is now. The following edited conversation between myself and Brian Holmes gives some historic context. The aim is for these ideas to become part of a wider design conversation as they are as urgent now as they were then.

Oliver Vodeb: Understanding of the communications environment, and a knowledge and mastering of communications approaches are crucial for citizens resisting corporations. Could we say that the most interesting communication approaches are often born within the sphere of conflict between commercial discourse and opposing activist, noncommercial discourse, since this is the space with the highest degree of communicational tension?

Brian Holmes: That was the great game that emerged in the nineties, when contagious, improvisational subvertising appeared on the walls and in the new electronic media, to challenge what seemed to be the totally dominant practices of global branding. The graphic designer and the streetparty revolutionary stood up against the advertising creative and the CEO, while the hacker clubs were launching their viruses into the coded heart of Microsoft. It's the stuff myths are made of. And it's still happening in extremely positive ways check out chainworkers.org [see ecn.org/chainworkers/chainw/english.htm], for example. But whether it's the most interesting approach depends a lot on what you mean by "communication." At a certain level culturejamming becomes a kind of virtuoso sport, declining into late Adbusters, and you start to see the mirror image relation between the two opposing teams, sparring for the excitement and prestige of manipulating people's emotions. Then the corporations start to produce truly grotesque things, like Shell going ecological in the wake of the Brent Spar controversy, or BP rebranding itself as "Beyond Petroleum" a whole complex of greenwashing strategies that Eveline Lubbers has documented in a recent book.

But at another level, as the game goes even further, a third actor tends to enter the picture: the State. Anxious to preserve their democratic legitimacy even while they give it all away to the transnationals, European governments had to find some kind of communicational strategy with respect to broad social movements. What they mostly do, via the declarations of the leaders, the police and the information services, is to pass off the demonstrations as a mix of fun loving kids and more responsible "concerned citizens," whose messages are extremely important in front of the cameras, and totally forgotten at the negotiating tables. They also have the dogs and the clubs at the ready if there's any chance for a fight, because that can always be addressed most effectively through the communications strategy of "wanton violence in the street," which is great for separating the black blocs from the good people. The effectiveness of this double strategy has become more apparent to many of those among the social movements, but it's very hard to respond coherently from below, because that would require a kind of coordination that freely associating movements just can't produce.

OV: The dominant, commercial discourse is co-opting communication approaches developed by the activists. It does so to neutralize their effect, to destroy the critique, but also because it wants to use activist communications approaches, which are very effective. Do you think it is possible to avoid that dynamic or are we talking about a never-ending process of co-optation on one side and innovation on the other?

BH: The best example of co-optation is probably something like "guerrilla marketing." Agencies found out that they could use light, intimate, casual material like stickers that would be fun to distribute, and in that way the target groups themselves could ensure the distribution. So it looks homemade, spontaneous, because it partly is. The idea is to operate on the level of rumor, of conversation, which is where public opinion actually forms. But the more this is done, the more demanding people become with respect to meaning. Anyone engaged in an autonomous, self-motivated activity knows exactly what the issues are, they can't be fooled. And they gradually extend their knowledge through society, by slow but certain means. So the struggle comes to focus over that half-conscious crowd in the middle, all those who in theory could be led by the right communications strategy either to a process or to a product, that is, either to an active role in a meaningful politics or to the simple purchase of a commodity.

For the ad industry, and more broadly, for the established powers, for all those who want us to continually "buy into" the contemporary form of society, I think the real struggle is to keep a majority believing that these attempts at co-optation really work on the others, that is. Because in private, huge amounts of people see through it. So you have literally millions of people wondering why co-optation is so effective on the others. I'd like to say that from there, it's only a short step before they dare to say that the Emperor is naked. But the problem would be to find people who could actually put on the political clothes without immediately making the same kind of travesty. Or, as some would say, the problem is going beyond representation and the statistical logic of mass communication.

OV: Recently a lot of focus has been on tactical communication. The term comes from Michel De Certeau's book "The Practice of Everyday Life," where De Certeau stated that popular culture is not a domain of texts or artifacts but rather a vernacular language of "ways of doing." Representations should be used, in a tactical manner. This means a fast and flexible communication with mostly DIY media, the ability to react immediately. But this is not all there is. The path the message travels seems to be of great importance too?

BH:　　The tactical theme is one of those great ideas or insights that have transmigrated from the 1970s to the vastly different conditions of today. I think the keywords are "spectacle" and "free association." What De Certeau was trying to point at, in a language between anthropology and poetics, were the millions of people outside all the functions and manipulations of so called "modern" society people beneath the technological radar, whose intimate thoughts followed patterns all their own, rich and sophisticated patterns that could be developed freely in a space that was palpable and present, warm and emotional, but essentially outside the consciousness industry. Everyday life, and the everyday imagination of the poor and the powerless, could then be seen as a "tactic" of resistance, escaping the strategies of the standardizing media.

　　Most anthropologists would probably have preferred that it stop right there, with the poor and the powerless and their curious, almost invisible freedoms. But De Certeau's readers in the aftermath of the 70s were mainly young people in or on the fringes of the universities, and they saw that beckoning finger of the tactical pointing at their own lives, their own ways of speaking, doing and imagining, which they dreamed as lying outside what had been recognized as the spectacle society. So small scale, do-it-yourself media or what Guattari called "postmedia" appeared as the necessary and missing link to extend the conversations, to touch other people freely and playfully, to form new associations.

　　In this process of improvising new media, a kind of rough-edged, half-finished, everyday artistry became the hallmark of life outside the standards. It's a matter of communicative intimacy, of leaving behind a public sphere that's been poisoned by publicity. Free association now takes on the almost psychoanalytic meaning of a ruse or a tactic for avoiding the norm, for escaping the censorship.

Information, even when it's journalistic, must be left open so the others can get in, and the best way to do that is to open your own imagination and practice to the unknown, to the imperfect and unschooled, to the inter-linking paths of singular exchanges. Everything is in these paths, whereby through their own conversations people regain that power to form a political opinion which I talked about before.

The amazing thing is how quickly it all went. The early nineties in Europe saw an extension of video art approaches to much larger numbers of people, who were interested in politics too, and not so concerned about the artistic niceties and distances that institutions impose. That was the crowd at the first Next 5 Minutes festival in Amsterdam, in 1993. Then straightaway came the Internet, and the video camera could be linked up to a one-to-one/one-to-many planetary distribution system. At this point, a kind of free association in the psychic sense was cast adrift on the net, and it made possible a whole lot of free associations in the anarchist sense, on the urban terrain which itself became a local stage in the spectacular and networked conflicts of globalization.

Free association in the movement of movements is a tactics of transversality, a way to enlarge the struggles without having to look for the statistical averages. The thing is to somehow take or follow this ongoing struggle between the spectacular and tactical to a higher level, to the level of pragmatically effective politics under antagonistic conditions.

OV: I remember at the Next 5 Minutes festival, in 2002 in Amsterdam, one of the very interesting things was the strategic debate about the future of the highly influential global independent tactical media network Indymedia*. To me, it was fascinating to see the fear of the Indymedia people that they have become a brand in the corporate sense. From the perspective of an independent media network, such as Indymedia, how important is the process of "branding"? By that I mean the tactical communication of the organization's symbolic capital in a direction of self-deconstruction, and with that, the creation of the necessary critical distance of one's own audience towards one's own medium. All this with the purpose of stimulating the audience's critical perspective.

BH: You said it! But everything you just described has just about nothing to do with the established practices of branding, which constructs identities, statistical targets, knee-jerk populations.

The woman at the N5M tactical festival who proposed branding Indymedia had worked for big NGOs like Greenpeace, and that was her argument, bigger is better. Impose a clear identity to get the job done. But the big NGOs have become a kind of counter example.

What is now clear to many is that under neoliberal governance, volunteer organizations are called into disaster areas to do the social work that the corporations don't want to pay for. Though some people within the humanitarian NGOs themselves are quite critical of this, their organizational form and the scales at which they operate make national and international agencies their only real partner. And so they are caught within the form of transnational governance that capital has done so much to create.

I mean no harm to the people who tend the world's wounds, but I do believe that if we ever want to get out of this damaging model of predatory globalization, if we ever want to bring back a notion and a realization of substantial equality – the right to food, health care, education, livelihood, and simply to peace – then we have to change the fundamental conditions of statistically averaged communication, which has proven its ability to successfully reproduce exactly the current form of society. A society that includes people only as passive consumers – of charity or whatever – while it simultaneously excludes other people as no more than trash. How do you resist the very logic of that society?

Indymedia was an experiment with the network structure, seeking to institute the possibility and reality of directly political relations between individuals and small groups, at what was formerly considered a "massive" scale. This in itself will hardly solve all the problems; but it may provide many people with a way back into social and political involvement and a public dimension of existence, from which all but the managerial classes are now deliberately alienated. That's why I'd say that one of the stupidest proposals I've heard in my entire life is that of branding Indymedia.

* The Independent Media Center (also known as Indymedia or IMC) is an open publishing network of activist journalist collectives that report on political and social issues. Following beginnings in London and Sydney during the 1999 Carnival Against Capital, the first Indymedia Media Center was founded to report on the protests against the World Trade Organisational Ministerial Conference in Seattle. Indymedia became closely associated with the global justice movement, which criticized neo-liberalism and its associated institutions. (en.wikipedia.org/wiki/Indymedia)

Brian Holmes is an art and cultural critic, writer and activist frequently collaborating with social movements. He now lives in Chicago where he currently focuses on work with ecology and rivers and science. Work in progress can be seen here: casariolab.art. Together with his partner Claire Pentecost they run the Watershed Art and Ecology gallery.

From: Jason Grant <██████@inkahoots.com.au>
Sent: Fri, Sep 4, 2020 at 4:20 PM
To: Steven Heller <██████@sva.edu>
Subject: A couple of queries

Hi Steven,

I'm doing some research on branding and picked up a copy of your 'Iron Fists'. I hugely appreciated your swastika book – a great untangling of the historical complexities. Brilliant research so engagingly presented. I admire it a lot.

Likewise I greatly appreciate the research behind 'Iron Fists'. However, with respect, a few things confused me about your conclusions, especially in comparison with 'The Swastika'.

You might agree that the commercial ascent of branding has seen increasingly grand claims about its origins and significance?

For example, I'm thinking of a 2015 Lipencott curated Design Museum show in London claiming the evolution of branding beginning as biological evolution itself: "Nature evolved a simple yet sophisticated language of branding. We quickly learned it, we had to, and still use this language today." Also that cave paintings "are an important demonstration of how our Homo Sapien ancestors were hard-wired to brand."

Isn't this a (pretty lazy) attempt by the industry to naturalise and 'inevitablise' a contemporary (neoliberal) phenomenon? Don't fight it - or even question it – it's inescapable?

While I'd agree there's a strong case for locating Nazism in the evolution of branding, and that there's certain parallels with your other totalitarian examples, I got a lot of conflation with basic human meaning making, myth making, symbol creation, personality cults, and propaganda. Were they really using "new branding strategies to sell their political messages"?

Doesn't conflating branding with these aspects of communication render the term meaningless? Isn't branding (in the sense we understand it today) a much more recent product of late capitalism?

Conversely, I'm always surprised by the resurgence in interest around corporate identity/ branding standards manuals and how they don't credit the *Organisationsbuch der NSDAP* as an antecedent – although of course there are differences. So I struggled with your statement that "Although the Nazis did not, as many have asserted, develop the archetypical corporate standards manual…"

Not "archetypical" perhaps, but surely *prototypical*? I'm curious about your definitive statement (without any explanation) here. Why did they not? To me the *Organisationsbuch der NSDAP* is a far stronger link to branding's DNA than the personality cults and propaganda of Mao, Mussolini and Stalin. And isn't denying that direct (as opposed to general) branding antecedent just laundering the ideological roots of a dehumanising communications methodology?

Would love to hear your thoughts on this.

cheers,
Jason

---

4 Sep 2020, at 6:58 am, Steven Heller <█████@sva.edu>

You might agree that the commercial ascent of branding has seen increasingly grand claims about its origins and significance?

I would say that branding has become an industry that transcends its fundamental origins and inflates its significance. But it is an accepted practice now to build a heritage and create importance for a product or idea.

For example, in a 2015 Lipencott curated Design Museum show in London visitors encountered claims about the evolution of Branding beginning as biological evolution itself...

Sounds interesting. A little too deep in the weeds for my taste. But I use the term and the pragmatics of branding and brands very loosely. It is creating the appearance or identity of something while conveying a message to an audience, people, community, whatever that can be positive or evil but never neutral.

Doesn't conflating branding with these aspects of human communication render the term meaningless? Isn't branding (in the sense we understand it today) a much more recent product of late capitalism?

No. I think branding is basically a neutral yet historical discipline that can be used, as said for good or evil and everything in between the poles. It began in the Capitalist sense in the late 19th century - it was associated with advertising. Now it's inflated as a tool, not conflated. It's a tool that has evolved.

...So I struggled with your statement that "Although the Nazis did not, as many have asserted, develop the archetypical corporate standards manual..."

They did not. The AEG under Peter Behrens was closer to the first. But I think you have to go back to individual industries to address how labeling, logos and advertising was used in concert. Coca Cola is the most recognizable brand in the world. They knew what they were doing. It was before the Nazis. The Communists developed the hammer and sickle before the Nazis. And the Cammera Rosa was a brand symbol before the Communists, etc., and further back and back.

*Not "archetypical" perhaps, but surely prototypical? ...
And isn't denying that direct (as opposed to general)
branding antecedent just laundering the ideological
roots of a dehumanising communications methodology?*

I guess if you want to make that claim, its as valid
as any. I don't think that it is more archetypical in my
book than, say, Italian Fascism. But it is an EXTREMELY
IMPORTANT signpost in the ways branding was and
is used decades after the war. But even before Hitler,
the U.S. branded itself in many ways that are being
challenged today as supremacist.

best
s

Sep 4, 2020 at 2:20 AM Jason Grant <█████@inkahoots. com.au>

Hi Steven,

Many thanks for getting back so quickly. I really appreciate your responses even though I deeply disagree with
most of them. I don't want to take up any more of your
time so I'll resist responding to all of your very generous
replies, except for a couple of general points.

I think framing branding as a 'neutral tool' is a serious
mistake. For example, no matter how it's used, for 'good'
or 'evil', it still commodifies and exploits relationships.
Aren't social relations being mined and remade by
branding?

And as a designer working in community, cultural
and activist spheres I have long noticed the disturbing
phenomenon of branding capturing even those organisations and ideas that are in direct ideological opposition.
It's a kind of neoliberal Trojan horse.

I can't see any of this as neutral – unless you consider our social and economic systems as neutral. I think the communications industries are now so invested in branding there just doesn't appear to be a viable alternative – it's the 'End of History' for mass communication.

Many thanks again Steven for your generous responses, and I hope perhaps we can one day meet in the post-Covid world and talk further.

cheers,
Jason

---

5 Sep 2020, at 12:55 am, Steven Heller <████████@sva.edu>

By neutral I mean that branding in and of itself is a tool of ownership and identity.

Branding cattle is cruel but it is not political. Branding slaves is cruel and inhumane. I think today's branding industry is somewhere in between.

Naming our children is branding. Surnames are branding. If you choose to look through a Marxist lens or a neo-colonialist lens the branding industry can be blamed for a lot of sins. But branding is not the exclusive province of neo-liberal capitalists or neo-fascist monopolists.

We can agree to differ on the nuances, but I am not a fan of branding as a means of manipulation through mythology or enslavement through narrative.

best
steve

Oct 6, 2020 at 10:06 PM Jason Grant <██████@inkahoots. com.au>

Hi Steven,

Really appreciate your assistance. Hope the return to teaching has gone well.

I'm trying to get to the bottom of a couple of facts around the history of brand manuals. You mentioned AEG and Coca-Cola, but I can't find any evidence of these companies introducing a published style guide/ manual before the Nazis (in 1936). I'm trying to pinpoint the specific date a manual of systematised, integrated public communication was first published. I'm not talking here about the instigation of corporate identity practices generally.

It would be fantastic if you had any links or names I can follow up towards evidence of anything earlier than this?

cheers,
Jason

---

7 Oct 2020, at 12:49 pm, Steven Heller <██████@sva.edu>

I do not. I'd guess that corporate identity manuals did not exist before the late 1940s or early 50s (I'm thinking specifically of Lester Beall in the US or one of the Swiss designers in Zurich or Basel). Conversely, I saw something that was close to a manual, but not quite, for Michellien.

I don't have anything that you're specifying for AEG but I'm 60% sure that Peter Behrens created one.

The Nazi guide was not a corporate manual but it came close. It was a handbook for all operations and party leadership.

Try Jesse Reed at Standards Manual. He may have a better answer.

Oct 7, 2020 at 1:19 AM Jason Grant <█████@inkahoots. com.au>

Thanks Steven. I've been in touch with the companies themselves and they don't seem to have the records unfortunately. I'm still following up with Coca-Cola though – can't believe they don't have something...

That's my thinking too, that the 40's and 50's were the earliest brand manuals for corporations. Though my thesis is that the totalising impulse and methodology of branding found one of its first systematically integrated published expressions with the Nazis' *Organisationsbuch der NSDAP*. Sure, it isn't exactly the same as contemporary manuals (I reckon many of which are actually more different from each other than the Nazi handbook is from a generic contemporary example), but I don't believe the differences warrant setting it aside as unrelated. Based on the available evidence, to my mind it's just one of the earliest versions. To me, claiming otherwise just seems like an overly forced distinction.

Apologies, I know you've got much better things to do than argue with an Australian designer. But I was also surprised at some of your claims in a previous email. For example, it's a very sad day if naming my children was indeed an act of branding. As repulsive as I find this idea, it confirms my critique, that increasingly there aren't many spaces left that branding hasn't colonised. Timeless intimate human acts are now being (superficially, falsely) claimed as intrinsic to a neoliberal ideology. I just read a comment from Ian Anderson (Designers Republic) who reckons "Identity is how you look. Brand is who you are." We've well and truly drunk the Kool-Aid! But I think this uncritical swallowing of market ideology needs challenging, not encouraging.

As for the claim that branding isn't political, isn't dismissing a critique as a "Marxist or neo-colonialist lens" just a way of avoiding the substance of the critique? If I criticise unequal gender power relations through the lens of feminism, does that mean you can dismiss the "sins" of sexism, for example?

I'd agree that branding isn't "the exclusive province of neo-liberal capitalists or neo-fascist monopolists" – but isn't this its genealogy? And isn't branding's contemporary "success" just the way capitalism works – everything solid melting into air? I can't but help see the constant denial of design's political agency as way of maintaining the status quo.

Anyway, my condolences for the current state of your politic. I can't imagine what it's like on the front line of Trump's madness over there. I watched the presidential 'debate' with my children (9 and 11 years old) and they just couldn't believe it. I (only half jokingly) told them that if they're ever caught behaving like the President of the United States of America, they'll be grounded for a year.

cheers,
Jason

Oct 7, 2020 at 8:09 AM Steven Heller < ██████@sva.edu>

I am a contrarian by nature. Perhaps one of the reasons I've written so much about fascist and nazi abuse of graphic design. Mind, body and behavior control is hard wired into the body politic – ancient and modern.

Naming children is a case in point. How many kids were "branded" after saints, prelates and kings – lords all.

I know at least three Jesuses. Nazi Germany allow a "preferred list" of names. The Soviets had their faves too (i.e. Traktor or Tractor). Even hippies and other "non-conformists" branded their children. My own real first name (which is still my legal name) has a branded side. Jews were originally "son-of..." At one point they were not allowed last/family names. Napoleon allowed Jews last names, which often branded them by their trades (i.e one of my family names was Metzger or butcher). Any name like Cohen or Koen meant a Jew descended from royalty (or the equivalent in biblical times).

In short, you're right about naming (as affiliation, brand and respect); And it works in reverse: who today would be named Adolf? And look how many Black men and women go for contractions of African names, etc. instead of their white slave names.

I've written a bit about this, got to find my notes.

best
s

---

7 Oct 2020, at 10:37 pm, Steven Heller <▆▆▆▆@sva.edu>

also thought these may be of interest:

https://www.printmag.com/post/the-daily-heller-pepe-the-frog-wronged-by-alt-right-made-whole-again

https://www.printmag.com/post/the-daily-heller-what-is-the-brand-of-the-year

https://www.printmag.com/categories/daily-heller

Oct 8, 2020 at 2:01 AM Jason Grant <███@inkahoots. com.au>

Thanks for those links Steven. Especially for the heads up regarding the Pepe doco.

My problem with your name example isn't that children's names are given due to an aspiration, or to honour a memory, or cultural affiliation or the like, but that this could now be somehow considered "branding". Naming children for these reasons is of course something that has always happened, but retrofitting branding here as some kind of ahistoric process just falsely paints it as inevitable.

I think that calling the naming of children "branding" does what George Lackoff refers to as framing – where market values squeeze out non-market values and an opponent's words draw you into their worldview. It's just branding colonising language.

And from this perspective (regarding one of your links) I'm not sure using consumer logos to promote a fundamental democratic process such as voting is a good idea. In spite of the fact that many Americans equate democracy with consumerism (and socialism with anti-Americanism), I'd argue that far from a "rekindling" it undermines the process as much as the Republicans' attempts at actual voter suppression.

cheers,
Jason

Oct 8, 2020 at 8:22 AM Steven Heller <███@sva.edu>

Jason

I'm enjoying your ripostes. I don't necessarily agree but they are stimulating thoughts in me.

Naming is indeed arguable. But you cannot deny that branding is a practice and NOW a trend that is, in part based on retrofitting. I am doing that, but I'm also looking at a brand as a fashion (it must be in the capitalist sense) that must perpetuate itself to survive. Naming is consciously or not (in the mind of some parents) a means of perpetuation. Or has Steve Heller once said "the total integration of branding into our everyday existence" or as another wise man has said "You are what you eat."

best
s

---

8 Oct 2020, at 10:51 pm, Steven Heller < @sva.edu>

Re: co-opting global brands for VOTE.

One can read a lot into this or unpack some too.

I choose to see it as simple satire or at least irony. Pure and simple.

But on a more linguistic/psycho neurological level: It forces a double take, which produces recognition. VOTING is an obligatory yet voluntary act. VOTE is a brand that triggers the act - maybe even triggers an involuntary response.

s

Oct 9, 2020 at 3:31 AM Jason Grant < @inkahoots. com.au>

Hi Steven,

I too wanted to read the logos as satire, but based on your intro and their context I couldn't see it.

Branding "is now a trend that is in part retrofitting". I do agree, like many crusades that appropriate a tenuous history to legitimise their existence. I'm thinking again of the Nazis' manipulation of ancient, classical and Roman cultures here. But it doesn't mean we have to take the claims uncritically?

I think what is being perpetuated with branding is just market values.

cheers,
Jason

---

10 Oct 2020, at 10:47 pm, Steven Heller <███████@sva.edu>

Hi Jason

Agreed.

Frankly, I am at once a captive and rebel of branding (as I am of advertising). I am critical and often write critically of both. But I also succumb to their allure as a major aspect of design history. The hippie in me despises commercial co-option and appropriation. The 70 year old in me is seduced by design as tool of marketing (commerce, religion. politics, etc.).

I also still marvel at the pure beauty and intelligence of many trademarks and logos. And I am fascinated by the historical implications of many too.

Paul Rand used to complain to me about critiques of his identity system for Westinghouse (as they were supporting the Vietnam War) (Another book I'd love to write is how corporations – well branded ones – supported the Nazis). He saw his work as serving a client not as promoting war. It all plays into the same ends.

Woolworths, a brand I remember well as a kid, fostered

Jim Crow but was ground zero for anti-segregation protests. What does the brand mean today? Other than a 5 + 10 cent store, it was the focal point for civil rights revolution. Brands or the products and businesses and organizations they represent can be viewed through different lenses, historically and ahistorically.

IBM was associated with the Nazis too, as were Coca Cola and Walt Disney and Ford Motors. No one and nothing is totally without sin.

s

Oct 15, 2020 at 1:32 PM Jason Grant <██████@inkahoots. com.au>

I'm with you there Steven. Like most graphic design practices my studio has long been commissioned to create symbols of collective identity. We see our challenge now though to propose an alternative to branding so that the organisations we support and work with (often community, cultural or activist) don't undermine their missions by communicating in ways that contradict their ethos.

There must be more than one way to connect with a public, to promote visibility and recognition, right? A way that isn't exploitative and predatory?

Along with its close cousins, coercive social media and surveillance capitalism, I think branding needs to be buried.

You mention Paul Rand's problem with Westinghouse which to me typifies designers' naivety in our relation to systems of power. He could only see himself as separate from the consequences of his design through the modernist myth of neutrality and objectivity.

You should definitely do that book. But to me it's not just a company's link to the Nazis in the past that is ugly, but the way they engineer mass communication in the present.

cheers,
Jason

Steven Heller was an art director at the *New York Times* for thirty-three years. Currently, he is co-chair of the SVA / NYC MFA Design / Designer as Entrepreneur program and writes Printmag.com's *Daily Heller* column. He is the author or coauthor of two hundred books on graphic design, satiric art, and illustration including *The Swastika: Symbol Beyond Redemption?* and *Iron Fists: Branding the 20th-Century Totalitarian State*. He lives in New York City.

Guess the Branding Agency:

A BRANDSPEAK QUIZ (PART 1)

01 A global leader in brand consulting and design, ▮▮▮▮ helps clients create agile brands that thrive in today's dynamic, disruptive marketplace. Our work enables top brands to stand for something while never standing still.

02 ▮▮▮▮▮▮ is a global brand strategy, innovation and experience firm. We use the power of creativity to transform business for the better. As a strategic and creative partner to large corporations, cultural institutions and startups, we work with our clients on complex brand and business challenges.

03 We are ▮▮▮▮▮ ... We combine creativity, craft and technology into ideas and experiences that improve people's lives. We put insight and imagination at the center of everything we do. To make brands that can't be ignored. To accelerate growth. To build better futures at scale.

04 ▮▮▮▮▮▮ is a next-generation brand agency built on a spirit of creative optimism. We believe in the power of creativity to improve the future of people and organisations. Our expertise includes brand strategy, identity, communications, and brand management.

05 We are ▮▮▮▮▮▮, a global agency creating transformative brands that move organizations, people and the world forward. We believe that brands have the power to move minds and improve our world. They connect people, ignite conversation and feed our imagination.

6 Forging iconic moves for brands through strategy and creativity. ▮▮▮▮▮ has been the world's leading brand consultancy, for over 40 years – having pioneered iconic work and forged many of the brand building tools that are now commonplace.

7 ▮▮▮▮▮▮ creates brands the world loves. We make every experience people have with your business meaningful. We build brands with purpose, brands that impact the lives of millions, and brands that last.

8 ▮▮▮▮ is a global brand agency using creativity to design a better future. We believe that in a world of rapid change, there has never been a greater need to future-proof brands. Brands that seek to be brave and challenge convention.

Guess the Brand:

A BRANDSPEAK QUIZ (PART 2)

Challenging conformity by empowering triangles in a sea of squares... Our Sensory Brand World approach puts motion at the heart so that digital platforms can break new ground with a cohesive sensory language.

The spirit of our founder has inspired a Sensory Brand World that informs the entire human experience. All assets now live and breathe our new creative principles. Quirks that were once frowned upon are now celebrated as a badge of distinctiveness.

A progressive DTC experience takes ███████ to new heights with meaningful hyper-personalised expressions that appreciate diversity among true Triangles in this often divided world.

We playfully leverage our distinctive ████████████ chunk asset to connect with seasons and cultural moments in an ownable and unmistakably ███████ way. Celebrating the quirks in those who matter most with a connected human experience from screen to store.

All of the brand's powerful equities come together to create a premium but playful selection of experiences that reward in new and exciting ways time after time.

Love & thanks from Jason to: Catherine, Oli, Thea & Lotta.

Love & thanks from Oliver to: friends and family.

Acknowledgments:
Freek Lomme, Jordan McGuire, Robyn McDonald, Lindsay Mengel, Clare McFadden, Brian Holmes, Steven Heller, Elaine Hill, Sandy Kaltenborn, Kevin Yuen Kit Lo, Clive Russell, Sébastien Marchal, Alec Dunn, Nicolas Maigret, Jonathan Barnbrook, Roderick Grant, Patricio Davila, Gabriella Wilson, Kernow Craig, Madeleine Clifford.

I agree with Jürgen Habermas, for whom the quality of social life depends on the intensification of communicative action, now that the public sphere is dominated by mass media and colonised by economic, administrative and disciplinary power. It is in relation to this idea of creating a more radically democratic public sphere – rather than a pseudo-public one – as a means of effecting social change, that I am interested in the visible and verbal sign systems by which we communicate: in understanding the practice of signification as a value system, as a representation of the complex relationships of social-historical conditions. This in turn means that I must be aware of the relationships within which work is constituted now that the interaction of institutions, commerce and disciplines has monopolised almost all systems of representation.

Jan van Toorn, *design's delight*, 010 publishers, 2006

Don't sell your conscience; don't sell your Conscience
As no money, no money, no money, no money, no money can buy good name
Good name is better than silver and gold
And no money, no money, no money, no money, no money can buy good name

William Onyeabor, *Good Name*, Wilfilms Records, 1983

Jason Grant is a designer and co-founder of Inkahoots Design. The Australian studio is widely known for its creative advocacy, activism and adventurous visual communication. He has lectured in design, typography and art theory at universities in Australia and around the world. He was born in New Zealand, has lived and worked in London, and now lives in Brisbane.

Dr Oliver Vodeb is an inter/extra-disciplinary designer, critical theorist, educator and student. He is the co-founder and principal curator of Memefest. The global network has been working on decolonising knowledge and the public sphere through research, education, and interventions since 2002. Oliver is an academic at RMIT School of Design, Melbourne. He has published extensively, regularly gives lectures and conducts workshops globally and has designed and directed public campaigns and interventions in various parts of the world. He was born in Germany, grew up in Slovenia and lives in Melbourne.